MOLASSES
inspirations

MOLASSES
inspirations

Joy Crosby

Formac Publishing Company Ltd.

Special Thanks to:
Dunstan Smith, Shelley Hamilton, Mary Brodkorb, Sara Ritchie, Stephanie Pointet, Suzanne Bailey, Lynn Swan, Sue Brown, Nora Wills and all those who tested, tasted and enjoyed these magnificent molasses recipes from our Best Canadian Chefs.

Formac Publishing Company Limited acknowledges the support of the Cultural Affairs Section, Nova Scotia Department of Tourism, Culture and Heritage. We acknowledge the financial support of the Government of Canada through the Book Publishing Industry Development Program (BPIDP) for our publishing activities.

Library and Archives Canada Cataloguing in Publication
Crosby, Joy
    Molasses inspirations / Joy Crosby.
ISBN 978-0-88780-749-7
    1. Cookery (Molasses). I. Title.
TX819.M65C77 2008   641.6'36   C2008-903848-7

Formac Publishing Company Limited
5502 Atlantic Street
Halifax, Nova Scotia B3H 1G4
www.formac.ca

Printed in China

contents

INTRODUCTION

For many Atlantic Canadians, molasses conjures up thoughts of comfort food. Tastes and smells of foods we ate while growing up elicit memories that are linked to various family traditions. Foods consumed for all the "high and holy" holidays — or just on a daily basis — remind us of dishes that were lovingly prepared in the past.

Cooks whose kitchens and larders were supplied simply with basic ingredients used molasses to produce wonderful treats for their families in the form of breads, beans or desserts. Molasses poured onto a plate and then sopped up with a thick slice of fresh homemade bread generously covered with butter provided the perfect ending to many a meal.

Thanks to north-south trading with the Caribbean, molasses from the far-off cane fields of the sunny West Indies was for generations the principal sweetener along the eastern seaboard, enriching our recipes with colour and flavour. Barbados was a favourite source of molasses for the Atlantic Region. From the early 1800s, schooners and brigantines fought wild winds and unpredictable weather to deliver an essential sweetener for our baking and cooking needs. Romantic visions of tall ships, their white sails "full up" and loaded to the gunwales with casks and puncheons of precious cargo, continue to engage our imaginations.

Molasses also made its way out west with loyal easterners who couldn't live without their favourite sweetener. Thanks to the Klondike Gold Rush, molasses travelled to the West Coast to delight westerners as a topping for their porridge or pancakes, on their pan-fried potatoes, in their campfire bean pots or simply in their coffee.

Today we continue to enjoy basic recipes that have traditionally been enhanced with molasses. Moreover, we now also use it in main-course recipes — in marinades, bombes, glazes and drizzles. Molasses appears on menus in the finest restaurants as a main ingredient, a rub, a marinade or as a sauce or topping. Contemporary chefs have recognized the distinctive flavour and unique qualities of molasses, and they have created new recipes around this key ingredient.

We are fortunate to have been introduced to molasses so long ago and to be able to share this delicious legacy that has evolved so smoothly over the years into the gastronomic delights created by our illustrious "Best Canadian Chefs" and presented here in this cookbook.

In their unique recipes, our chefs massage our palates with ingredients from around the world, such as tamarind, jackfruit and lemongrass, which are all used in combination with molasses to create a marvelous synergy. Their creations bombard our senses with aromas, tastes, textures and visual presentations.

How far we have come from recipes in our great-grandmother's cookbooks calling for "butter the size of an egg" to a chef's very memorable dessert caramelized with the use of a culinary blowtorch.

TYPES OF MOLASSES

The type of molasses you use is a matter of personal preference.

FANCY MOLASSES

is the pure juice of the sugar cane, condensed, inverted and purified. It is the highest grade of molasses available, 100 percent natural and contains no additives or preservatives such as sulphites. It is light in colour and tangy-sweet.

BLACKSTRAP MOLASSES

is the residual liquid obtained in the manufacture of refined sugar. The purified cane juice is concentrated into a thick mass. As the sugar crystallizes, this mass is passed through a centrifuge, which separates the mother liquor from the crystallized sugar. The resulting molasses is very dark and has a robust, somewhat bitter flavour. It contains no added sulphates or sulphites.

COOKING MOLASSES

is a blend of blackstrap and fancy molasses that can be used in baking and sauces, licorice candy, beans or for fermentation.

LIGHT MOLASSES

is a product made from fancy molasses plus glucose-fructose and other ingredients, and is formulated to be reduced in calories.

CULINARY USES OF MOLASSES

Molasses is a wonderful, natural and inexpensive flavour enhancer and sweetener, which masks bitter flavours and is a great accompaniment to herbs and spices. It is a natural colourant of great stability and makes an ideal substitute for brown sugar, artificial brown colouring, cocoa powder, butterscotch, caramel and so on. Blackstrap molasses is often used in meat or vegetable dishes as a sweetener and colouring agent. The liquid consistency of molasses eliminates the lumping and clumping frequently encountered with other sweeteners or colourants.

In baking, molasses acts as a leavening agent. The natural acids in molasses react with baking soda to produce gas, which enhances the spring and texture of baked goods. Cooking molasses may be used when baking bread, however the bread may not rise as high as with fancy molasses. Blackstrap molasses is also used in a variety of baked goods. In addition, molasses is a natural humectant — it prolongs the shelf life of baked goods by helping them retain moisture.

NUTRITIONAL AND HEALTH VALUE

Molasses is fat-free and cholesterol-free. Molasses is also gluten free and is safe for people with celiac disease. One tablespoon (15 mL) of fancy molasses contains 65 calories. One tablespoon of blackstrap molasses has 56 calories and also contains 20 percent of the daily recommended intake of iron, as well as significant amounts of calcium, magnesium, potassium and vitamins B2 and B6. For these reasons it is often considered a health food.

STORAGE AND SHELF LIFE

Molasses has a shelf life of 12 to 18 months. It does not require refrigeration. If you do keep molasses in the refrigerator, the old expression "slow as cold molasses" applies — it will be much slower to pour. Also, over a period of time in the refrigerator, the sugars may crystallize.

SOUPS, STARTERS AND SALADS

The first course is the one that whets the appetite and establishes the tone of the whole meal. The starters presented here range from the simple to the sublime, but they have one thing in common: they are all delicious.

Some of the dishes are as elaborate as a meal — but in miniature, of course. Many of them present a stunning visual feast. You won't be disappointed with the beautifully golden Caramelized Butternut Squash Soup, the bite-sized Shrimp in Tempura with Mango and Molasses Dip or the eye-catching Jackfruit and Molasses Barbecue Sauce on Nova Scotia Calamari. If foie gras is your passion you will be dazzled by the Foie Gras and Candied Apple Stack, a presentation from the kitchen of Chef Eric de Montigny.

These starters are not only beautiful to look at, but also delightful to eat, and a perfect kick-off for any meal.

LA BOHÈME MOLASSES CREPES

La Bohème Restaurant B & B, Edmonton, AB

Crepes are versatile and can add a light touch to any part of your menu. They freeze beautifully and can be brought out magically and used to dazzle your guests with sweet or savoury fillings.

These savoury crepes, with a small amount of filling, are a perfect appetizer but can also be used for brunch or lunch. Chef Adil Abouizza uses buckwheat to give them a mild, earthy mushroom flavour. In addition to its many health benefits, buckwheat is gluten free and can be enjoyed by anyone with gluten sensitivities.

Crepes

    1 cup (250 mL) buckwheat flour
    1 egg, beaten
    2 tsp (10 mL) walnut oil
    1 ¾ cups (435 mL) milk
    2 tbsp (30 mL) molasses

Combine all ingredients and stir well to create a smooth batter. Pour 2 to 3 tablespoons of batter into a small non-stick skillet that has been brushed lightly with oil. (Use a small ladle to achieve crepes of uniform size). Swirl pan to spread batter thinly. When dry on top, flip crepe over and cook for another 15 to 20 seconds. Place on a rack to cool. Once cooled, the crepes can be stacked, prior to using, with waxed paper between them.

Filling

    2 tsp (10 mL) walnut oil
    2 tsp (10 mL) water
    4 cups (1 L) uncooked baby spinach (stems removed)
    1 ½ cups (375 mL) chopped asparagus tips, cooked *al dente*
    2 whole green onions, finely chopped
    1 egg, beaten

    1 egg yoke
    ¼ tsp (1 mL) nutmeg
    1 cup (250 mL) cottage cheese
    ½ cup (125 mL) walnut pieces, finely chopped
    ¼ cup (60 mL) sharp cheddar, grated

In a large non-stick skillet, add walnut oil, water, baby spinach, asparagus tips and green onions. Cover and cook on medium heat, shaking periodically, until spinach has reduced. Add beaten egg, egg yolk and nutmeg to pan and stir quickly. When egg is done, add cottage cheese and walnut pieces. Stir to blend and remove from heat.

To serve, place crepe with best side down and spoon filling in a line down the centre. Add a sprinkle of sharp cheddar and fold over. Arrange on a serving platter and decorate with edible flowers and chive greenery.

Makes 8 crepes

MOLASSES AND SOY-GLAZED SEA SCALLOPS

Saint John Ale House, Saint John, NB

Chef Jesse Vergen uses a Japanese soy sauce that has a somewhat sherry-like taste. It also contains wheat, making it slightly sweeter than Chinese soy. The infused flavours of soy sauce, sesame oil and orange zest give the scallops a lovely Asian zing. They can be served as an appetizer or on a spring salad.

1 cup (250 mL) molasses
6 ½ tbsp (100 mL) Japanese-style soy sauce
5 tsp (25 mL) sesame oil
1 tsp (5 mL) orange zest
20 sea scallops
sea salt
cracked black pepper

Mix molasses, soy sauce, sesame oil and orange zest in a bowl and let the flavours of the glaze develop overnight. Preheat broiler. Reserve about one quarter of the glaze. Marinate scallops in remaining glaze for 10 minutes, then remove and season with salt and pepper. Place under broiler for 3 minutes, then remove from oven. Brush scallops with a little more glaze and finish broiling for another 3 minutes. Brush scallops with reserved glaze when done.

Serves 4

FOIE GRAS AND CANDIED-APPLE STACK

Le Bistro, Montreal, QC

This dish is perfection itself. Chef Eric de Montigny is a skilled master who has created a visual masterpiece that will also dazzle your taste buds. The stacked flavours of the sweet apple with a hint of tartness, the distinctive colour and texture of the pumpernickel bread, the smooth and rich foie gras — all topped with caramelized butter and molasses — are diverse and tantalizing. To top it all off Chef de Montigny serves warmed applesauce as a condiment. Foie gras can be specially ordered from your butcher.

> 17 to 21 oz (500 to 600 g) foie gras (Grade C or better)
> milk (enough to cover foie gras)
> 1 tsp (5 mL) four-spice (cinnamon, nutmeg, ground clove and allspice mixture)
> salt and pepper
> 4 Braeburn apples
> 1 ½ tbsp (22 mL) sugar
> 1 loaf black Russian bread or Pumpernickel
> ½ lb (225 g) unsalted butter, cubed
> 4 cloves garlic
> several sprigs fresh thyme
> 2 tbsp (30 mL) blackstrap molasses
> *If serving fresh warmed applesauce as a condiment, allow 5 Courtland apples.

Marinate foie gras in milk in an airtight container for 24 hours, to soften the flavour and draw out the remaining blood. (This step will give the best results, but it is not essential.) Remove foie gras from milk, rinse under cold water and pat dry. Cut into four to six 1 inch (2.5 cm) thick medallions. Season medallions with half the amount of four-spice and salt and pepper and place them in the refrigerator, uncovered.

Slice off the top and bottom of the apples and remove their cores (preferably with an apple corer). Cut each apple horizontally into three even rings, about 1 inch (2.5 cm) thick. Place apples in a bowl and add a light seasoning of salt, remaining half of the four-spice and sugar and toss. Allow apples to stand for about 10 minutes to soak up the salt and sugar. Slice bread into 1 ½ inch (3.75 cm) thick square pieces and trim to about the same size as the apple rings.

In two ovenproof frying pans over medium heat, divide butter cubes into even amounts, and melt but do not brown them. Place foie gras, 2 garlic cloves and half the fresh thyme in one pan and allow it to brown gently for 5 minutes on each side. Remove from the pan and place on a paper towel to soak up excess fat. Place squared bread slices in the same pan and toast each side. Remove and place on a paper towel.

Place apple slices, remaining garlic cloves and fresh thyme in the other pan. Using a spoon, drizzle molasses over apples and into butter and caramelize each side evenly. Reduce the heat to avoid burning sugar and molasses, as this will result in a bitter flavour. When apples are tender, remove and place on a paper towel.

To assemble the stack, place a slice of apple and then a piece of bread in the centre of a plate, followed by another piece of apple. Top with foie gras. Drizzle remaining butter and molasses caramel from the apple pan over the stacks.

Serves 4 to 6

BLUE CHEESE, PEAR AND ANISE SALAD WITH SHERRY-MOLASSES VINAIGRETTE

Gabrieau's Bistro, Antigonish, NS

This is a delightful salad with a mix of greens and an abundant supply of surprises – cheese, pears, shaved fennel, candied nuts – even hot spice if you want. Candied nuts are simple to make and are certainly the pièce de résistance of Chef Mark Gabrieau's creative and inventive salad, which is simply divine.

Sherry-Molasses Vinaigrette

1 tbsp (15 mL) Dijon mustard
5 tbsp (75 mL) sherry vinegar
1 tsp (5 mL) lime or lemon juice
1 tbsp (15 mL) diced shallots
1 tsp (5 mL) minced garlic
¾ cup (185 mL) extra-virgin olive oil
1 tbsp (15 mL) each, fresh tarragon, parsley, chives and chervil
2 tbsp (30 mL) molasses
pinch of salt and crushed pepper

Mix all ingredients together. Pulse in a blender, food processor or hand blender.

Salad

1 cup (250 mL) baby arugula
1 cup (250 mL) radicchio
1 cup (250 mL) sliced Belgium endive
1 cup (250 mL) baby spinach
2 cups (500 mL) shaved anise bulb
½ cup (125 mL) thinly sliced red onions
2 cups (500 mL) thinly sliced pears
1 to 2 cups (250 to 500 mL) crumbled blue cheese (or other cheese of your choice)

Toss lightly and add desired amount of candied walnuts or pecans (recipe follows)

Candied Walnuts

2 to 3 cups (500 to 750 mL) molasses (enough to cover nuts)
2 cups (500 mL) walnuts or pecans

In a pot on medium heat, place molasses and nuts and bring to a boil, then simmer for 3 minutes. Remove pot from heat and strain nuts. Place nuts on a baking sheet lined with parchment paper or a silicone baking mat and bake in 350°F (180°C) oven for 8 minutes or until nuts appear somewhat frothy and dry. Cool nuts, then break apart and store in an airtight container until required. To give the nuts a "kick," you can sprinkle them with Cajun spice after straining but before baking.

Serves 6 to 8

MOLASSES AND CARAMELIZED-ONION SLAW

Oscar's, Barrie, ON

Chef Rachael Whitman has created a staple with this divine molasses and caramelized onion dressing, which takes on a totally different flavour depending on how you use it.

Some of the chef's other suggested uses for this dressing are trying it with a salad of arugula greens, toasted walnuts, pomegranate seeds and smoked chicken. It makes a great sauce for shrimp, chicken and pork and also a terrific spread for a sandwich with any filling you might fancy.

This rich, delicious salad is easy to prepare. Fresh herbs make such a difference, so don't be afraid to experiment with the quantity of the thyme. Jicama comes from South America and is also recommended. It resembles a squashed beige turnip. It has the same properties as a water chestnut and remains firm in soups so it is a terrific addition to your favourite veggie soup or in a stir fry.

Slaw

- 1 cup (250 mL) carrot
- 1 cup (250 mL) jicama (jicama is found quite readily in the produce section of most grocery stores but if unavailable, shredded red or white cabbage could be used)
- 1 cup (250 mL) snow peas
- ½ cup (125 mL) tart apple (2 medium apples)
- 1 cup (250 mL) celery root
- ½ cup (125 mL) toasted sunflower seeds
- 1 cup (60 mL) onion sprouts for garnish
- 4 snow peas for garnish
- 1 cup (250 mL) Molasses and Caramelized-Onion Dressing (recipe follows)

Julienne the vegetables using a mandolin, a food processor or simply grate by hand.

Molasses and Caramelized-Onion Dressing

- 2 red onions, finely sliced
- 2 tbsp (30 mL) butter
- 2 tbsp (30 mL) oil
- 1 tsp (5 mL) puréed garlic
- ½ cup (125 mL) molasses
- 2 cups (500 mL) mayonnaise
- chopped fresh thyme
- 1 tsp (5 mL) sherry wine vinegar
- salt and pepper to taste
- lemon juice to taste

Sweat onions with butter and oil in a frying pan on medium heat, constantly tossing until they are soft and translucent. Wait until they start to brown (caramelize), turn down the heat and cook until the mass of onion has become evenly brown. Browning the onions concentrates the natural sugars and intensifies the flavour of the dressing. Add puréed garlic, leaving it in the pan long enough to cook through, but not burn. Set aside to let cool. Add molasses, mayonnaise, thyme and vinegar and stir until well combined. Season with salt, pepper and lemon juice to desired taste. This dressing can be refrigerated for up to 1 week.

Toss together all slaw ingredients with molasses/onion dressing to desired moistness. This dressing is so delicious that a dressing dispenser can be put on the table so your guests can help themselves to more if needed.

Serves 4 to 6

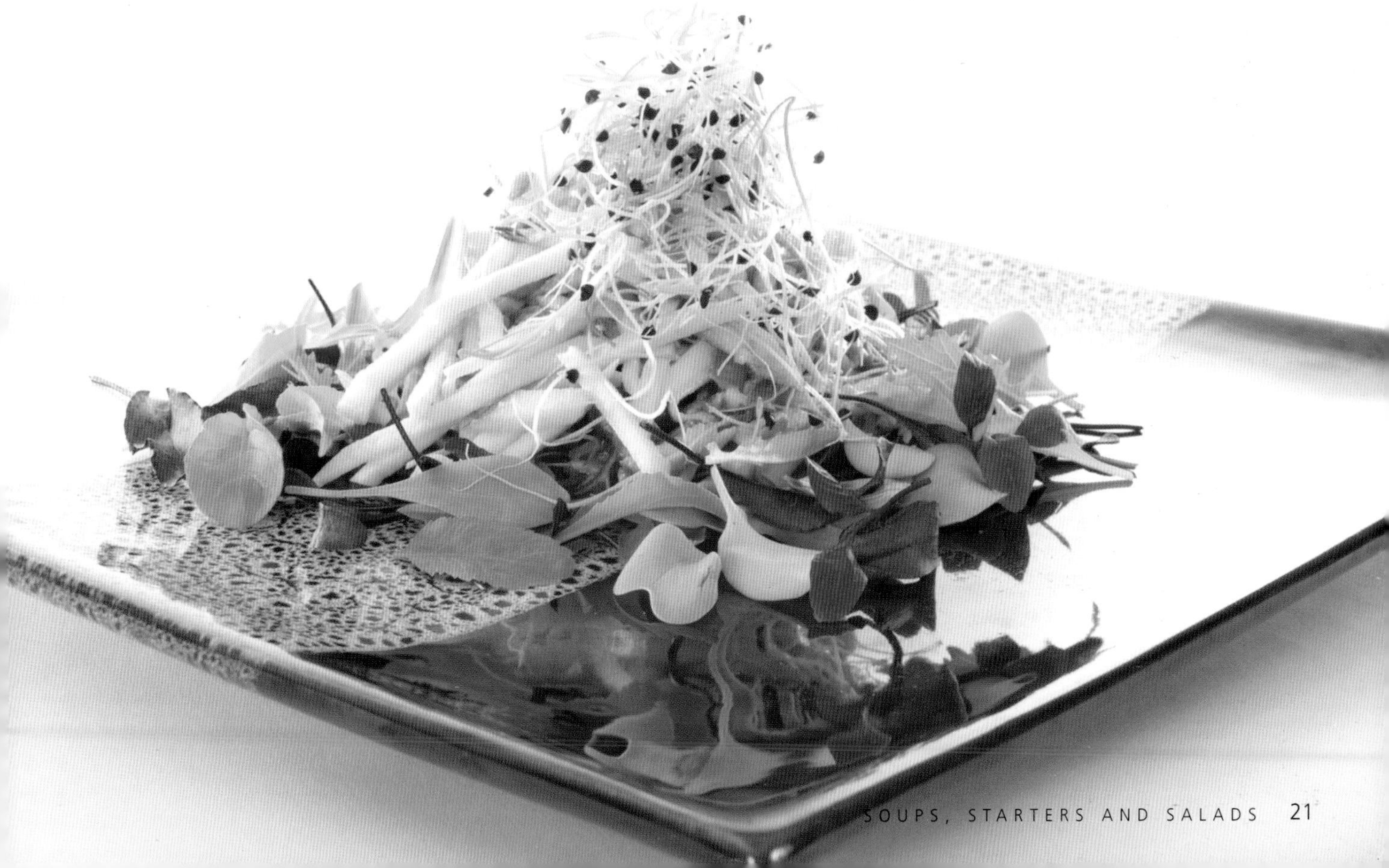

LEMONGRASS AND MOLASSES-CANDIED SALMON

Mojo, Regina, SK

Chef David Straub finds this recipe extremely versatile because the candied salmon can be used for many different dishes. It is wonderful in salads, canapés and even simply on its own as an appetizer or main course, and can be served either warm or chilled.

The syrup can also be used for many dishes. It adds great punch to barbecue sauces, dressings or dipping sauces for fish. It also makes a great glaze for duck and other game meats. This is definitely a staple for your recipe collection.

Lemongrass Molasses Syrup

2 stalks lemongrass (use only about the first 6 in or 15 cm of stalk)
1 cup (250 mL) water
1 cup (250 mL) brown sugar
3 tbsp (45 mL) molasses

Remove outer dried leaves of lemongrass and discard. Lightly pound stalk (to release aromatic flavours) with a rolling pin or meat tenderizer, then chop coarsely. In a heavy sauce pan, add lemongrass, water, brown sugar and molasses. Bring mixture to a boil and simmer for 10 to 15 minutes or until syrup coats the back of a spoon. Remove from heat and cool completely. Remove stalks of lemon grass. Refrigerate at least 2 hours to allow syrup to set.

Candied Salmon

4 x 8-oz (225 g) salmon fillets
1 cup (250 mL) lemongrass syrup

Preheat oven to 400°F (200°C). Line a roasting pan with parchment paper or tin foil coated liberally with non-stick spray. Place fillets of salmon in pan and cover with syrup. Bake in the oven for 15 minutes, basting salmon with syrup every 5 minutes. Remove from oven and let stand 10 minutes. Carefully remove salmon fillets to a container, discard pan drippings and chill completely in refrigerator before using. The salmon will last for one week and the syrup will last for 6 months in the refrigerator.

Serves 4

CARAMELIZED BUTTERNUT SQUASH SOUP

Opera Bistro, Saint John, NB

Butternut squash becomes deeper in colour and sweeter and richer in flavour as it ripens. Its sweet, nutty taste, combined with fresh ginger and ground pepper creates an exquisite soup. Chef Margaret Begner says that her soup is suitable either as an appetizer or as a light lunch or supper, served with a thick slice of hearty multigrain bread and a dollop of sour cream.

> 1 medium butternut squash, seeded, peeled and halved
> 2 cups (500 mL) water
> ¼ cup (75 mL) butter
> 1 tbsp (15 mL) brown sugar
> 3 tbsp (45 mL) molasses
> 3 cups (750 mL) vegetable stock
> salt
> ground black pepper
> finely chopped fresh ginger, to taste
> sour cream, for garnish

Preheat oven to 400°F (200°C). On a baking sheet, place squash halves with the cut sides facing down. Add about ½ inch of water to baking sheet and roast for 45 minutes, until squash is tender. Remove baked squash from its skin and set aside. In a pot, melt butter and add brown sugar and molasses. Bring to a simmer, keeping a close eye on it so that it doesn't burn, then turn the heat off. Add squash and vegetable stock and purée. Stir frequently as you are heating the soup so it doesn't stick. If soup is too thick, add some water or more vegetable stock. Adjust seasoning with salt, pepper and fresh ginger. Garnish with sour cream.

Serves 4 to 6

CREOLE BEEF SKEWERS

Cathedral Freehouse, Regina, SK

Chef Matt Johnstone is surrounded by dynamic decor from local artists and strives to achieve the same artistry in his menu. These skewers are full of robust good taste and perfectly adorn the salad drizzled with the delicious creole mustard sauce. They are lip-smacking good.

Creole Mustard Sauce

1 ⅓ cup (335 mL) Dijon mustard
¼ cup (60 mL) molasses
½ cup (125 mL) mayonnaise
2 tbsp (30 mL) white wine vinegar
2 tsp (10 mL) Worcestershire sauce
½ cup (125 mL) minced onion
¼ cup (60 mL) minced tomato
¼ tsp (1 mL) turmeric
¼ tsp (1 mL) freshly ground pepper
1 tsp (2 mL) fresh thyme
1 tbsp (15 mL) minced fresh garlic

Mix all ingredients well to make a creamy sauce and reserve half of marinade for the beef. Put the other half into a squeeze bottle for the topping.

Salad

½ cup (125 mL) diced, cooked sweet potatoes
2 tbsp (30 mL) sliced green pepper
2 tbsp (30 mL) sliced yellow onion
2 tbsp (30 mL) sliced celery
½ tomato, cut into quarters

In a bowl, mix all ingredients together.

Lemon Thyme Dressing

3 oz (90 mL) fresh lemon juice
1 cup (250 mL) extra virgin olive oil
1 tbsp (15 mL) sugar
2 tsp (10 mL) salt
1 tsp (5 mL) freshly ground pepper
1 oz (30 g) fresh thyme

Rub the fresh thyme between your fingers to extract the aromas then shake all the ingredients together in a glass storage jar. Shake again before serving on the salad

Beef Skewers

1 lb (450 g) beef loin
fresh thyme, for garnish

Marinate beef loin for 2 hours or more in Creole Mustard Sauce. Cut into 1 inch cubes and thread onto 4 skewers. Grill until beef is medium-rare.

To serve, toss the salad with lemon thyme dressing and place in pasta bowls. Add a beef skewer on top of salad and squeeze a zigzag of creole mustard sauce over entire dish. Garnish with fresh thyme.

Serves 4

JACKFRUIT AND MOLASSES BARBECUE SAUCE ON NOVA SCOTIA CALAMARI

Gio, Halifax, NS

Jackfruit is the national fruit of Bangladesh and Indonesia, and it is the highlight of this recipe. The unique marriage of jackfruit and molasses is a perfect accompaniment for any fish but, Chef Ray Bear particularly recommends it for Nova Scotian calamari (squid). He prepares both a grilled and a shallow-fried version of the calamari. It absolutely melts in the mouth, and the vibrant flavour of the jackfruit will win you rave reviews.

Calamari

  2 lb (900 g) mixed calamari (heads and tails)
  buttermilk (enough to cover calamari in airtight container to tenderize)
  1 cup (250 mL) fine bread crumbs
  1 cup (250 mL) flour
  1 tbsp (15 mL) salt
  canola oil (enough to fill your frying pan up to 1 inch for shallow frying)
  juice of one lemon
  two lemons, cut into wedges to use for garnish

Soak calamari in buttermilk overnight to tenderize them. Cut off the tails if necessary. Mix together bread crumbs, flour and salt. Coat half of the calamari and shallow fry lightly for about 1 ½ minutes or until edges curl slightly. If overcooked, calamari can become tough. Cut remaining calamari lengthwise and cut the insides lightly with a sharp knife for tenderness. Place on a hot grill for about 1 minute to achieve good grill marks. Sprinkle calamari with lemon juice and roll them up for presentation.

Serves 4

Jackfruit and Molasses Sauce

  ¼ cup (60 mL) canola oil
  1 lb (450 g) jackfruit*, flesh sections only
  4 plum tomatoes, peeled and seeded
  ¼ cup (60 mL) peeled whole garlic
  3 shallots, peeled and halved
  1 tbsp (15 mL) finely chopped fresh ginger
  3 to 5 green finger peppers, seeded and veined (quantity depends on desired hotness)
  1 cup (250 mL) red wine vinegar
  juice of 2 limes
  2 cups (500 mL) light molasses
  ¼ cup (60 mL) fresh basil, chopped
  ¼ cup (60 mL) fresh cilantro, chopped
  1 tbsp (15 mL) smoked paprika
  salt to taste
  * Use canned jackfruit if fresh is hard to find. It is available at any specialty green grocer or most Asian and East Indian grocery stores. Because of its large size, fresh jackfruit is sold in wrapped wedges.

Heat a large, heavy-bottomed saucepan to medium-high temperature. Add oil, jackfruit, tomatoes, garlic, shallots, ginger and peppers and cook until jackfruit is caramelized and shallots are transparent. Mix in the remaining ingredients and allow to simmer slowly for 20 minutes. Purée the sauce and check for seasoning. Add salt as needed. Serve immediately or cool and store in a sealed container in the refrigerator for up to 5 days.

Yields 3 to 4 cups

MOLASSES-GLAZED ROASTED VEGETABLES

Aux Vivres, Montreal, QC

These glazed veggies are a treat for breakfast, lunch or supper. Chef Michael Makhan serves them with other leafy greens, cooked or raw, to round out the meal.

Molasses Glaze

½ cup (125 mL) extra virgin olive oil
½ cup (125 mL) balsamic vinegar
½ cup (125 mL) molasses
½ cup (125 mL) water
4 tbsp (60 mL) fresh rosemary
1 tsp (5 mL) black pepper
1 tbsp (15 mL) salt
2 tbsp (30 mL) fresh garlic

In a bowl, mix all ingredients well.

Vegetables

3 large sweet potatoes, peeled and cubed
6 large white potatoes, washed and cubed
4 large carrots, peeled and chopped
2 small white onions, peeled and chopped
2 parsnips, peeled and chopped
2 leeks, washed and chopped

In a pot of boiling water, blanch all vegetables for 10 minutes. Drain.

Mix blanched vegetables with glaze in a bowl. Bake at 350F (180C) for 25 minutes on an oiled roasting tray, until golden.

Serves 6 to 8

SHRIMP IN TEMPURA WITH MANGO AND MOLASSES DIP

Garçon!, Montreal, QC

This is a tart and sweet treat that is truly fantastic. Chef Gérôme Lefils has created a colourful sauce with mangos and molasses in which to dip these delicately wrapped shrimp. The pink pepper adds just enough zip to the dip.

24 large shrimp, $^{16}/_{20}$*, cooked
2 shallots, finely chopped
2 tsp (10 mL) pink pepper
1 tsp (5 mL) olive oil
2 tsp (10 mL) white vinegar
2 tsp (10 mL) lemon juice
4 tsp (20 mL) molasses
¾ cup (200 mL) mango purée
salt and pepper, to taste
premixed Tempura flour (Available anywhere that Sushi is sold. Follow instructions on the box and change flour halfway through.)
ice
lemon oil to taste
canola oil to cover bottom of wok or deep frying pan to shallow fry shrimp
* $^{16}/_{20}$ refers to the size of the shrimp and represents the quantity per pound (16 to 20 shrimp per pound)

Peel shrimp and keep refrigerated. For the dip, sweat shallots and pink pepper in olive oil. Add vinegar and lemon juice and reduce by half. Add molasses and mango purée, bring to a boil and add salt and pepper to taste. Place in an automatic mixer and mix, then strain the mixture and let it cool.

In a bowl, following the instructions on the Tempura package, mix ice-water, Tempura flour and lemon oil. Stir to moisten but batter will be lumpy. Coat shrimp with tempura batter and deep-fry. Drain shrimp and season with salt to taste. Serve with dip.

Serves 6

WINTER SALAD WITH ROASTED-SHALLOT AND MOLASSES VINAIGRETTE

Joy Bistro, Toronto, ON

The salty goodness of cheddar cheese adds substance to this delicious combination of greens, grapes and molasses-caramelized apples. Chef Bryan Burke tops it off with the rich mellow sweetness of the roasted shallots in the vinaigrette. You have a salad that will please even the most discerning palate.

Winter Salad

½ lb (225 g) organic spring mixed greens
¼ cup (60 mL) crumbled old white cheddar
¼ cup (60 mL) halved red grapes
¼ cup (60 mL) halved green grapes
¼ cup (60 mL) Molasses-Caramelized Apples (recipe follows)
3 tbsp (45 mL) Roasted-Shallot and Molasses Vinaigrette (recipe follows)

Combine all salad ingredients and mix delicately so as not to bruise the lettuce. Divide evenly onto individual plates or wooden bowls.

(½ cup [125 mL] each of the cheddar, red and green grapes and caramelized apples can be used if a richer and fuller salad is desired.)

Serves 4 to 6

Molasses-Caramelized Apples

2 tbsp (30mL) sugar
2 tbsp (30mL) butter
2 (two) medium-sized Ontario apples
1 tbsp (15 mL) molasses

In a heavy-bottomed small pan, sprinkle sugar. Heat over medium low heat until sugar turns a pale amber colour. Add butter and mix until melted. Cut apples into small wedges (about 16 pieces), add them to the pan and toss with sugar. Cook for about 1 minute and turn each piece of apple over. Add molasses and cook for another 2 minutes. Let cool. Add evenly to each salad serving.

Roasted-Shallot and Molasses Vinaigrette

2 shallots
3 cloves garlic
2 tsp (10 mL) fresh thyme
2 tbsp (30 mL) molasses
2 tsp (10 mL) grainy mustard
½ cup (125 mL) red wine vinegar
½ cup (125 mL) sunflower oil or grape seed oil
salt and pepper to taste

In a small ovenproof dish, place shallots, garlic, thyme and molasses. Roast at 325°F (165°C) for approximately 20 minutes, or until shallots are soft. In a food processor, combine shallots with mustard and vinegar. Purée for a few seconds while adding the oil. Season with salt and pepper to desired taste. Drizzle to taste on salad. Vinaigrette can be refrigerated for up to a week

Yields 1 cup

BREADS

Not a day should go by without fresh bread. It is truly the staff of life — just ask the French.

Our Canadian Chefs have shared their best bread recipes. We are particularly pleased that the Blomidon Inn has generously given us the recipe for the bread that they make daily.

Whether you're looking for a fabulous basic recipe, a nutty nosh or a cornbread, one of these bread recipes will satisfy your needs.

BLOMIDON INN BREAD

Blomidon Inn, Wolfville, NS

Dining at the Blomidon Inn would not be complete without a slice of this delicious bread. Chef Sean Laceby is proud to share it with us. The combination of oats, cornmeal and molasses give it a rich and dense flavour with stick-to-the-ribs goodness.

1 cup (250 mL) oats
½ cup (125 mL) cornmeal
1 ¼ cups (310 mL) molasses
½ tsp (2 mL) salt
2 cups (500 mL) hot water
¼ cup (60 mL) shortening
1 cup (250 mL) warm water
3 tbsp (45 mL) yeast
½ tbsp (7 mL) sugar
7 cups (1.75 L) all-purpose flour
cooking spray

Stir together oats, cornmeal, molasses, salt, hot water and shortening and let mixture cool to a lukewarm temperature. In a separate mixing bowl, stir together the warm water, yeast and sugar. Let yeast soften until slightly foamy then stir to ensure that it is properly dispersed.

In a food mixer, add oat mixture to yeast mixture and mix at speed # 1 until homogeneous. Turn off mixer and add flour to make a firm — but not dry or sticky — dough. The quantity of flour depends upon the temperature of the mixture. The best method is to add half the quantity, then turn on the mixer (speed #1) and mix until uniform. Slowly add enough of the remaining flour until there is a good dough mass in the mixer — one that comes clean from the mixer walls but is not dry. Knead the bread for an additional 3 to 5 minutes until the flour has been worked in uniformly and the dough is more elastic.

Separate dough into 22 oz (625 g) portions and shape into loaves. Use cooking spray on the bread pans and on the dough to keep bread from sticking to the pans. Let rise until the dough mass forms good-sized loaves (about 1 inch, 2.5 cm above the pan). This usually takes about 60 to 75 minutes. Bake at 350°F (180°C) until loaves sound hollow when tapped. The baking takes about 25 to 30 minutes. Remove from pan and cool on a cooling rack.

Makes 2 loaves

OATMEAL AND FLAX SEED BREAD

Mojo, Regina, SK

Chef David Straub developed this recipe a couple of years ago and it has become one of the signature breads at Mojo. It is served at lunch for menu items such as house-cured pastrami Reuben's, roasted pear and Brie sandwiches and Marsala roasted duck sandwiches. At night it is served in croustini form for fish and vegetarian dishes. It has the comforting element of olden-day prairie cooking.

2 cups (500 mL) warm water
2 tbsp (30 mL) yeast
1 tbsp (15 mL) sugar
¼ cup (60 mL) butter, at room temperature
2 eggs
½ cup (125 mL) molasses
1 cup (250 mL) rolled oats
¼ cup (60 mL) ground flax seed, or ½ cup (125 mL) whole flax seed
6 cups (1.5 L) all-purpose flour

Preheat oven to 350°F (180°C). In a mixing bowl, combine water, yeast and sugar. Stir gently and let stand for 10 minutes. Once the yeast has bloomed, add butter, eggs and molasses. Whisk well to combine. Add oatmeal, flax and half of the flour and stir until the mixture has thickened slightly. Add remaining flour and knead for about 10 minutes on a floured surface. Form dough into a ball, cover with a damp cloth and allow to rise in a warm spot for about 30 minutes. Punch the dough down to deflate it, divide in half and form into two logs. Rub two bread pans with butter or oil. Place dough in pans, cover with a damp cloth and let stand to rise again until doubled in size. Bake bread in oven for 30 minutes (bread is done if it sounds hollow when tapped). Remove from oven and cool on a wire rack.

Makes 2 loaves

MOLASSES CORNBREAD

Shadow Lawn Inn, Rothesay, NB

Chef Darren Bennett's cornbread is delightful in flavour and texture, is easy to make and can be served with a meal or simply with a spot of tea. If served hot, there is nothing better than scooping up a dollop of butter and a pool of molasses from your plate.

1 tbsp (15 mL) butter, to grease loaf pan
1 ¼ cups (310 mL) all-purpose flour
2 ½ tsp (12 mL) baking powder
¾ tsp (4 mL) salt
¼ tsp (1 mL) baking soda
1 ¼ cups (310 mL) yellow cornmeal
3 tbsp (45 mL) sugar
1 ¼ cups (310 mL) milk
¼ cup (60 mL) molasses
1 large egg
1 ¼ sticks or 10 tbsp (150 mL) unsalted butter, softened

Preheat oven to 400°F (200°C) and butter a 9 x 5 x 3 inch (22.5 x 12.5 x 7.5 cm) loaf pan. In a large bowl, sift together flour, baking powder, salt and baking soda and whisk in cornmeal and sugar until combined well. In a separate bowl, whisk together milk, molasses and egg until just combined. Add butter to flour mixture and with an electric mixer beat until mixture resembles fine crumbs. Beat in milk mixture until just combined. (Do not over mix.) Pour batter into pan and bake in middle of oven for about 35 minutes, or until a tester comes out clean. Cool in pan on a wire rack for 10 minutes then turn bread out onto the rack to cool completely. Cornbread may be made 2 days ahead and kept in plastic wrap in a cool, dry place.

Makes 1 loaf

DATE, MOLASSES AND WALNUT BREAD

Bacchus, Vancouver, BC

Chef Lee Parsons is a master at creating sensory appeal and this bread is a real treat. Walnuts and dates, in combination with molasses, enrich both the taste and the texture.

⅔ cup (165 mL) dried dates
¾ cup (190 mL) molasses
5 tbsp (75 mL) walnut oil
1 ¼ cups (300 mL) warm water
2 tbsp (30 mL) fresh yeast
3 ½ cups (875 mL) wholemeal flour
2 ½ tbsp (40 mL) salt
⅔ cup (165 mL) walnuts

Soak dates, molasses, water, walnut oil and yeast together for 2 hours at room temperature. Add flour and salt and knead until smooth. Cover with damp cloth and let dough rise in a warm spot to twice its original size. Knock it down and add walnuts. Shape to desired size, put in two greased pans, cover with damp cloth and let it rise again to double the size. Bake at 350°F (180°C) for 25 to 30 minutes (to determine doneness, tap on bottom of bread & if it sounds hollow, it's done). Remove from pan and let cool on wire rack.

Makes 2 loaves

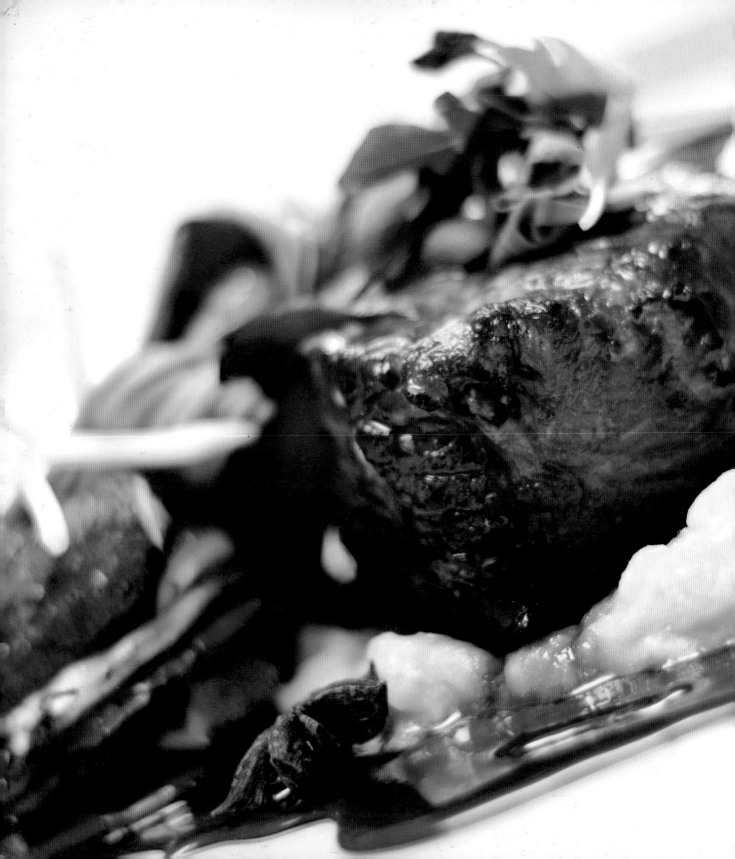

ENTRÉES

The main course is the foundation on which the menu is built, and all bases are covered with this varied sampling of main-course fare.

Our featured performer, molasses, can add a special oomph to seafood, poultry and meat. Molasses as a flavour can present itself in rich warm undertones, as a deeply colourful sauce or make a full-blown appearance in caramelized apples. In these recipes it is highlighted in marinades (Molasses and Sake Marinated Sablefish); glazes (Fire-Roasted Chicken with Tamarind-Molasses Glaze); and infusions (Tomato and Molasses-Braised Lamb Shanks), demonstrating a few of our Best Canadian Chefs' sensational dishes.

Whatever the occasion, you will find a delicious main course here to delight your dinner guests.

MOLASSES AND SAKE MARINATED SABLEFISH (ALASKAN BLACK COD)

Feenies, Vancouver, BC

Chef Jasmin Porcic is not afraid to experiment, and this fusion of molasses, miso and sake as a marinade for the sablefish is a winner. Sablefish has a very high oil content, so it needs to be exposed to high heat.

The recipe works equally well with salmon or halibut. The shiitake mushrooms and bok choy, combined with the Yukon potatoes and fresh ginger, give this dish a truly "east meets west" flavour. Bonito flakes (dried, fermented and smoked skipjack tuna) and combu (seaweed) are available at any Asian store and are the main ingredient of Japanese sauces and soups, such as miso. Chef Porcic recommends pairing this dish with any Riesling, which is clean and crisp to balance the sweetness of the molasses.

2 tbsp (30 mL) sake
2 tbsp (30 mL) water
½ cup (125 g) of fresh miso
¼ cup (60 mL) molasses
2 tbsp (30 mL) soy sauce
4 pieces sablefish, each 6 oz (170 g)
1 cup (250 mL) Yukon Gold potatoes, cubed
1 cup (250 g) bok choy
1 tsp (5 mL) olive oil
½ cup (125 mL) shiitake mushrooms
white pepper, to taste
1 ½ tbsp (20 mL) grated ginger
⅓ cup (90 mL) Dashi Broth (recipe follows)
chopped chives, as garnish

Bring sake and water to a boil. Remove from heat and let sit for 20 minutes, then add miso until fully dissolved. Add molasses and soy and mix over medium heat. Let cool. Marinate sablefish in refrigerator for 12 to 16 hours. When ready to cook, remove fish from marinade (do not rinse), place on a baking dish and bake for 10 minutes in a 400°F (200°C) oven. The fish is ready when it starts flaking. Blanch potato cubes in boiling water until they are soft but still retain their shape. Remove and reserve. Blanch bok choy and reserve. In a frying pan, heat olive oil and sauté shiitake mushrooms. When mushrooms are soft, add fresh grated ginger, potatoes and bok choy and heat through. Season with white pepper to taste.

Place vegetables in a large serving bowl. Add fish on top of vegetables and pour boiling Dashi Broth over the fish. Garnish with chopped chives.

Dashi Broth
    4 cups (1 L) water
    ⅓ cup (85 mL) soy sauce
    ½ cup (125 mL) bonito flakes
    1 piece combu
    chili flakes, to taste

Bring water and soy to a boil. Add bonito flakes and remove from heat for 15 minutes in order for flavours to infuse. Add combu and bring back to a boil. Add a few chili flakes to perfume the broth. Combu can be removed before serving. Serve evenly over potatoes, bok choy and fish and garnish with chopped chives.

Serves 4

SCALLOPS ON SAFFRON AND MOLASSES RICE

Glynn Mill Inn, Corner Brook, NL

Chef Joe Froud's scallop dish is easy to prepare and the rich, sweet goodness of the molasses and butter perfectly enhance the deeply flavourful scallops. The large chunks of colourful peppers are pleasing to the eye and counterbalance the subtle colour of the rice. This dish will be a big hit with seafood lovers.

2 cups (500 mL) basmati rice
¼ cup (60mL) clarified butter*
4 to 5 sprigs of saffron (optional if unavailable — saffron adds a lovely colour and flavour)
1 cup (250 mL) molasses
2 tbsp (30 mL) dark brown sugar
5 cups (1 ¼ L or 1250 mL) water
2 lbs (900 g) jumbo sea scallops
4 shallots, cleaned and quartered
1 each, large red, green and yellow peppers, diced
fresh parsley, as garnish
lemon wedges, as garnish

*To clarify butter: Melt butter in a saucepan over medium heat until milk solids separate. Remove milk solids. Remaining liquid is clarified butter and will not burn.

Wash and dry basmati rice and sauté in half the clarified butter until lightly browned. Mix together molasses and brown sugar and add half to the rice. In a large saucepan, add 5 cups water and cook on high heat until rice comes to a boil, reduce heat to low and cook until done. Do not stir. Watch for bubble holes in top of rice and tip pot to make sure all water is gone.

In a large skillet, sauté scallops with remaining clarified butter, shallots, peppers and remaining molasses/brown sugar mixture. Fluff rice and place in a bowl. Pour scallops and vegetables over the top. Garnish with fresh parsley and lemon wedges.

A curl of lemon rind can also be added for a more artistic flair.

Serves 6 to 8

MOLASSES, GRAPEFRUIT AND SAGE-BRINED BREAST OF FREE-RANGE CHICKEN

The Harvest Room, Edmonton, AB

Chef David Wong says that by combining molasses and grapefruit juice in the brine for the chicken, he can create the perfect sweet and sour environment: the vibrant flavours are retained and both the marinade and the natural juices are absorbed and sealed in. The risotto is flavourful and the combined plate is intensified with the addition of a grapefruit jus (sauce).

This dish also goes well with pan-roasted fingerling potatoes and, of course, fresh seasonal veggies for colour. A dry Riesling is the ideal wine pairing.

> 2 cups (500 mL) grapefruit juice
> 1 cup (250 mL) molasses
> 6 sage leaves
> ¼ cup (60 mL) kosher salt
> 4 cups (1 L) water
> 6 free-range chicken breasts
> Parmesan Risotto (recipe follows)
> Grapefruit Jus (recipe follows)

Bring brine ingredients to a boil, turn off heat and let cool. Marinate chicken breasts in brine for 8 hours then slow roast in an oven at 275°F (135°C) until done. Serve with Parmesan Risotto.

Parmesan Risotto
> 2 shallots, minced
> 2 cloves garlic, minced
> 2 tbsp (30 mL) unsalted butter
> 2 tbsp (30 mL) vegetable oil
> 2 cups (500 mL) Carnoli or Arborio rice
> salt and white pepper, to taste
> 1 bay leaf
> ½ cup (120 mL) white wine
> 12 cups (3 L) chicken stock
> ¼ cup (60 mL) grated fresh Parmesan cheese

In a large pot over medium heat, sweat shallots and garlic in melted butter and vegetable oil for 5 minutes. Add rice and stir to coat in fat. Season the mixture with salt and white pepper and stir gently by shaking the pot (use a wooden spoon sparingly, as this will break the grains of rice). Add bay leaf and wine and cook until there is no aroma of the wine, ensuring that you do not brown the rice. Add hot chicken stock, ½ cup (120 mL) at a time, until half of each addition is absorbed. This will ensure a creamy risotto. The risotto is done when the rice is *al dente*. Remove bay leaf, add Parmesan cheese and re-adjust seasoning.

Grapefruit Jus

- 1 shallot, minced
- 1 clove garlic, minced
- 1 tbsp (15 mL) butter
- 1 cup (250 mL) white wine
- 1 cup (250 mL) grapefruit juice
- 1 tbsp (15 mL) sherry vinegar
- 1 tbsp (15 mL) molasses
- 4 cups (1 L) chicken stock
- 4 tbsp (60 mL) unsalted butter salt to taste

Sweat shallot and garlic in butter. Deglaze with wine and reduce by half. Add grapefruit juice and reduce again by half. Add sherry vinegar, molasses and chicken stock and reduce until mixture reaches a sauce-like consistency. Whisk in unsalted butter and season with salt to taste. Pour over risotto and chicken breasts and garnish with curled grapefruit rind and parsley.

Serves 6

FIRE-ROASTED CHICKEN WITH TAMARIND-MOLASSES GLAZE AND ASIAN COLESLAW

Cabot Club (Fairmont, St. John's, NL)

Tamarind packs a powerful taste for such a little tropical nut. Its distinctive flavour perfectly compliments the molasses in this sauce. Chef Roary MacPherson serves it with chicken, but it can also be used for beef, pork or fish. It makes an excellent light lunch.

> 4 bone-in chicken breasts, skinned
> 4 chicken thighs, skinned
> Tamarind-Molasses Sauce (recipe follows)
> ½ cup (125 mL) olive oil to brush on chicken pieces
> salt and freshly ground pepper, to taste

Marinate chicken in the sauce for 2 to 3 hours. Remove chicken, brush with oil, season with salt and pepper and place on a preheated grill. Grill for 6 to 7 minutes on each side, or until golden brown and cooked through. Brush chicken with sauce during cooking. Remove from the grill and brush with more sauce.

Serve with an Asian coleslaw (recipe follows) and pommes frites (French Fries).

Tamarind-Molasses Sauce
> 2 tbsp (30 mL) unsalted butter
> ½ cup (125 mL) finely diced onion
> 2 cloves garlic, finely diced
> 6 plum tomatoes, coarsely chopped
> ¼ cup (60 mL) tomato paste
> ¼ cup (60 mL) water
> 2 tbsp (30 mL) Dijon mustard
> 2 tbsp (30 mL) dark brown sugar
> 4 tbsp (60 mL) molasses
> 2 tbsp (30 mL) tamarind concentrate
> 1 tsp (5 mL) cayenne
> 1 tbsp (15 mL) chili powder
> 1 tbsp (15 mL) paprika
> 1 tbsp (15 mL) Worcestershire sauce

In a large saucepan, heat butter over medium-high heat. Add onions and garlic and cook until soft. Add remaining ingredients and cook for 15 minutes. Place mixture in a blender and blend until smooth. Return to the saucepan and cook for an additional 15 to 20 minutes, or until thickened.

Asian Coleslaw:
> ½ cup (125 mL) green cabbage, julienned
> ½ cup (125 mL) snow peas, julienned
> ¼ cup (60 mL) green onion, sliced
> ½ cup (125 mL) carrots, julienned
> ½ cup (125 mL) napa cabbage, julienned
> 1 tbsp (15 mL) chopped cilantro
> 1 cup (250 mL) bean sprouts

Mix all ingredients together.

Asian Sesame Dressing:
> ½ cup (125 mL) mayonnaise
> 1 tbsp (15 mL) apple cider vinegar
> 1 tbsp (15 mL) white vinegar
> 1 tbsp (15 mL) sesame oil
> 1 tsp (5 ml) dried garlic
> 1 tbsp (15 mL) roasted sesame seeds
> salt and pepper to taste

Whisk all ingredients together in a bowl and mix gently into the coleslaw, being careful not to break the bean sprouts.

Serves 4 to 6

PORK TENDERLOIN WITH MOLASSES GLAZE AND CARAMELIZED APPLES

Victoria Village Inn, Victoria-by-the-Sea, PEI

Chef Stephen Hunter's combination of molasses and spices creates a pork dish that melts in the mouth and is enhanced by the crowning glory of the caramelized apples.

> ½ cup (125 mL) molasses
> ½ cup (125 mL) malt vinegar
> ½ tsp (2 mL) allspice
> ½ tsp (2 mL) garlic powder
> ½ tsp (2 mL) ground ginger or ½ tbsp (7 mL) grated fresh ginger
> 1 tsp (5 mL) chili powder
> 2 whole pork tenderloins, halved
> salt and pepper
> 1 tbsp (15 mL) cooking oil
> ¼ cup (60 mL) dry white wine
> Caramelized Apples (recipe follows)

Whisk together molasses, vinegar, allspice, garlic, ginger and chili and divide into two portions. Reserve one portion for the Caramelized Apples. Preheat oven to 350°F (180°C). Dry the pork tenderloin and season with salt and pepper. Add oil to a large ovenproof frying pan over high heat. When oil just starts to smoke, add pork tenderloin and sear for 1 minute. Turn pork to sear other side, then remove from heat. Add wine to half of the molasses glaze and baste the pork to coat. Place frying pan in the oven and roast for 20 minutes or until pork is cooked medium-well. Remove pork from pan and drizzle any remaining pan juice over it.

Serve Caramelized Apples over pork.

Caramelized Apples

> 2 tart green apples, peeled, cored, and cut into wedges
> reserved molasses glaze
> 1 small onion, cut into thin wedges
> 1 tbsp (15 mL) cooking oil
> ¼ cup (60 mL) dry white wine

Toss apple wedges in reserved molasses glaze. In a medium sauté pan, fry onion in a little cooking oil until browned. Remove apples from the glaze, add them to the pan and sauté for 2 minutes. Add wine and continue to sauté until wine has almost all evaporated.

Serves 6 to 8

PAN-SEARED AHI TUNA WITH A MOLASSES AND ORANGE SAUCE

Maestro S.V.P., Montreal, QC.

Chef Yves Therrien has created this fabulous seafood extravaganza with the surprise flavours of dark rum and orange. The tuna is exquisitely blended with famous southern ingredients, which compliment it magnificently. Bravo maestro.

¼ cup (60 mL) minced French shallots

¼ cup (60 mL) olive oil

½ cup (120 mL) Xéres vinegar (sherry vinegar or white wine vinegar can be substituted)

½ cup (90 mL) frozen concentrated orange juice

6 tbsp (90 mL) molasses

1 tbsp (15 mL) minced ginger

2 tbsp (30 mL) dark rum

2 pieces of tuna, 6 oz (170 g) each

salt and pepper

1 orange, segmented

In a non-stick pan, heat shallots in olive oil until they are clear. Deglaze pan with Xéres vinegar and reduce by half. Add all remaining ingredients except orange segments. Let simmer for 5 minutes.

In a separate black steel* pan on high heat, pan-sear tuna lightly on both sides until cooked to your liking. (Medium rare is recommended. Tuna is best cooked to a light colour on the outside and left red on the inside as it gets tougher the longer you cook it.)

To serve, cover tuna with sauce and decorate with orange segments. Serve with steamed carrots, asparagus and small potatoes.

*Black Steel is an ideal and affordable pan that is perfect for cooking fish as it doesn't stick.

Serves 2

JUMBO SHRIMP IN MOLASSES MARINADE

Chez Bruno, Yarmouth, NS

Chef Bruno Sieberath has an eye for colour and the option of using red Thai rice is spectacular. A terrific combination of fire from the chillies and tartness from the lime enhances the shrimp, but this marinade can be used with any seafood available to you.

    1 tsp (5 mL) rubbed red chillies
    1 cup (250 mL) molasses
    3 tbsp (50 mL) fish sauce
    ⅓ cup (80 mL) lime juice
    ¼ cup (60 mL) white wine vinegar
    3 tbsp (50 mL) chopped garlic
    5 lb (2.25 kg) tail-on jumbo shrimp, peeled
    5 tsp (25 mL) chopped coriander
    10 tsp (50 mL) sliced green onions
    2 cups red Thai rice or basmati rice
    baby bok choy and carrot slivers

Mix together chillies, molasses, fish sauce, lime juice, vinegar and garlic and marinate shrimp for 15 to 20 minutes. Remove shrimp from marinade and cook on a hot grill for one minute on each side. In a pot, reduce marinade until it is syrupy, then reduce further to a glaze and add coriander and green onions.

Serve over red Thai rice (cooked according to package instructions) or cooked basmati rice (2 ½ cups water to 1 cup of rice) with sautéed baby bok choy and sautéed carrot slivers. Drizzle with sauce and sprinkle with fresh coriander.

Serves 6 to 8

MARINATED PORK PINWHEEL

Personal Chef to the Lieutenant-Governor of New
Brunswick, Fredericton, NB

*Chef Rob Agar's combination of molasses, red wine
and lemongrass in his marinade adds pizzazz and
freshness of flavour. The addition of cranberries to the
basmati rice stuffing adds colour and texture. The pork,
with its interwoven flavours, is exquisite to the eye and
pleasing to the palate. It goes well with grilled
asparagus and sliced grilled red peppers. Chef Rob
Agar also suggests serving this pork dish with a
ratatouille.*

  1 cup (60 mL) molasses
  1 cup (60 mL) red wine
  1 shoot lemongrass
  1 tsp (5 mL) salt
  1 tsp (5 mL) fresh pepper
  2 tbsp (30 mL) minced fresh ginger
  1 pork tenderloin, trimmed
  1 ½ cups (375 mL) cooked basmati rice
  ½ cup (125 mL) dried cranberries
  salt and pepper to taste
  chives, as garnish

Combine marinade of molasses, red wine, lemongrass
(crushed with back of a knife to release the flavours),
salt, pepper and ginger and stir together well. In a loaf
pan, cover pork with the marinade for at least 5 hours,
turning every hour or so. Remove loin and slice it along
the side, turning it slightly with every incision, from
one end to the other so it can be stuffed. Combine
enough of the marinade (pieces of lemongrass can be
removed at this point) to flavour and moisten the
cooked basmati rice and the dried cranberries. Spread

the filling evenly on the rolled-out loin, packing it
down as you go. Roll up the loin tightly and tie it
with string or butcher's twine. In a skillet with oil, sear
all sides of the meat then roast in an oven at 400°F
(200°C) for about 15 minutes. Reduce the remaining
marinade in a pan and pour over the sliced
tenderloin, reserving a little for plating.

To serve, slice tenderloin on the bias and fan out on
the plate with vegetables of your choice in the middle
and sauce on top. Garnish with two long chives
planted in the veggies.

Serves 4 to 6

RICOTTA GNOCCHI

Capo Restaurant, Calgary, AB

In Southern Italy, it is common practice to make gnocchi with a mix of ricotta and potatoes. However, Chef Giuseppe Di Genarro uses only the ricotta, as he finds it makes the dumplings fluffier and softer. It also gives them a more pronounced cheesy flavour.

This gnocchi, with the combination of molasses and bacon, hits you with a sweet and salty taste that's hard to beat. Buono appetito!

>   2 cups (500 mL) all-purpose flour
>   2 cups (500 mL) ricotta cheese
>   1 egg
>   salt and pepper
>   Butter Sauce (recipe follows)

In a large mixing bowl, form flour into a well. Mix ricotta with egg and add to the well. With a circular motion, fold flour into the ricotta a little at a time, until all the flour is exhausted. Add salt and pepper to taste. Wrap with plastic wrap and chill for at least ½ hour. Flatten dough and cut into strips lengthways. Roll strips into long dowels (like a wooden dowel in a chair back) to the thickness of your choice and cut into (1 inch long) small dumplings with a sharp knife. The number of servings depends on how large or small you cut the gnocchi. Refrigerate until ready to use.

Sauce
>   ¼ cup (60 mL) smoked bacon lardoons
>   ¼ cup (60 mL) unsalted butter
>   1 cup (250 mL) shitake mushrooms
>   1 shallot, finely diced

Topping:
>   ½ cup (125 mL) grated Parmiggiano Reggiano cheese
>   ¼ cup (60 mL) fancy molasses
>   salt and pepper to taste

Place the bacon and butter in a pre-heated skillet. Let the butter brown and the bacon render by half. Add the mushrooms and shallots and cook for 3 to 4 minutes. Season and set aside. Boil gnocchi in plenty of salted water until all the dumplings rise to the surface and float (remove immediately so they won't get tough). Drain and add to the hot sauce. Finish by topping with grated cheese and a good drizzle of fancy molasses. Serve hot.

Serves approximately 4 to 6

MOLASSES SAKE JACKFISH

The Dandelion Eatery, Winnipeg, MB

This fish is spectacularly delicious and colourfully presented with yellow and red peppers. Chef Ben Kramer recommends you serve it with a salad of organic greens so that both your flavour and your health needs will be more than satisfied.

  1 cup (250 mL) sake
  3 tbsp (45 mL) maple syrup
  ¼ cup (60 mL) molasses
  4 x 6-oz jackfish (northern pike) fillets
  3 tbsp (45 mL) grapeseed oil
  1 yellow pepper, sliced
  1 red bell pepper, sliced
  1 leek, diced
  6 tbsp (90 mL) white wine
  2 ½ cups (625 mL) fish stock
  2 tbsp (30 mL) molasses
  salt and pepper

Mix together sake, maple syrup and molasses and marinate jackfish fillets for 2 hours, then remove from marinade. In a hot sauté pan, add grapeseed oil and sauté jackfish until brown on both sides. Remove fish from pan and finish cooking in a lightly oiled roasting pan in a 400°F (200° C) oven for about 3 to 5 minutes, or until done.

In the sauté pan, add peppers and leeks and sauté until tender. Deglaze with white wine and reduce by two-thirds. Add fish stock and molasses and reduce by one-quarter. Season with salt and pepper.

Serve with organic greens and boiled fingerling potatoes.

Serves 4

SWEET MOLASSES-SMOKED TENDERLOIN

Tavern in the Park, Winnipeg, MB

*Chef Joe Dokuchie offers this combination of beef
tenderloin, wasabi potatoes, vegetable timbale and
sauces to dazzle your senses. There are many steps and
a lot to learn in this recipe but the variety of flavours
make this a powerful plate fit for a king and a
guaranteed show-stopper. It is well worth the effort.*

> 2 lb (900 g) beef tenderloin, cleaned (centre cut only)
> For the brine:
> 4 cups (1 L) water
> 3 cups (750 L) sugar
> ¼ cup (60 mL) salt
> ¼ cup (60 mL) molasses
> ½ tbsp (7 mL) minced garlic (2 cloves)
> 2 pieces star anise
> ¾ tsp (4 mL) cracked peppercorns
> ¾ tsp (4 mL) cracked whole allspice berries
> ¼ tsp (1 mL) cumin
> ¾ tsp (4 mL) whole coriander
> ¾ tsp (4 mL) chilli flakes
> ½ tbsp (7 mL) cilantro fakes, dried

Mix all brine ingredients together and bring to a
simmer, then cool completely. Submerge tenderloin in
brine in a large roaster and weigh down with a couple
of plates. Refrigerate for 24 hours. In a hot smoker
unit, smoke for 45 minutes to 1 hour until tenderloin is
rare to medium-rare. Serve with Wasabi Mashed
Potatoes, Asian Vegetable Timbale, Veal Syrup and
Dijon Emulsion (recipes follow).

Wasabi Mashed Potatoes
> 6 Yukon Gold potatoes, peeled
> 2 tbsp (30 mL) salt
> 2 tbsp (30 mL) butter
> 1 tbsp (15 mL) wasabi paste
> 2 tbsp (30 mL) butter (second amount)

> 1 tsp (5 mL) salt
> pinch white pepper
> pinch nutmeg

Simmer potatoes in water seasoned with salt and
butter. Once potatoes are tender, mash in a small
mixer and add remaining ingredients. Form into
quenelles using two tablespoons.

Asian Vegetable Timbale
> 1 rib of celery
> 2 carrots
> 1 yellow zucchini
> 1 green zucchini
> 1 leek (white part only)
> 1 red onion
> ¼ cup (60 mL) sesame oil
> 1 tsp minced garlic
> 1 green savory cabbage, fresh
> 1 tbsp (15 mL) salt
> sesame oil to taste, to be added to water when
>   cooking cabbage

Julienne celery, carrots, zucchini, leek and onion on a
mandolin or with a sharp knife. In a hot pan, add
sesame oil, garlic, onion, carrot and celery. Season
with salt and pepper. Sauté until just soft. Add
zucchini and leek and season again. Sauté until
zucchini is just limp. Refrigerate.

To make timbale packages, separate leaves of
cabbage. Cook in salted boiling water with a bit of
sesame oil until leaves are very tender. Pat dry with
paper towel and then remove heavy centre rib.
Arrange cabbage leaves in 6 to 8 2 inch (5 cm)
timbales and fill with vegetables. Reheat in a
microwave for 1 minute when ready to serve.

Veal Syrup

4 cups (1 L) brown veal stock
roasted tenderloin scraps
¼ cup (60 mL) red cooking wine
¼ cup (60 mL) marsala wine (Italian portlike amber wine)
1 tsp (5 mL) peppercorns, crushed
½ cup (125 mL) mirepoix (chopped onions, celery and carrots)
2 pieces star of anise
1 tbsp (15 mL) cold butter

In a skillet over medium heat, combine all ingredients (except the cold butter) and reduce by a third, stirring constantly. Strain. Return to stovetop and bring to a boil. Remove from heat and whisk in the cold butter. The cold butter adds rich flavour and also makes the sauce thicker and gives it a bit of shine. (This technique is called *beurre monte*.)

DIJON EMULSION

1 shallot, minced
2 cloves garlic, minced
salt and pepper
¼ cup (60 mL) red wine vinegar
2 tbsp (30 mL) molasses
1 cup (250 mL) canola oil
2 tbsp (30 mL) grainy Dijon mustard

Sauté shallot and garlic and season with salt and pepper. Add red wine vinegar and molasses. Purée in blender with canola oil, then whisk in Dijon mustard. Place in a squeeze bottle. Garnish plate with emulsion.

Plating Instructions:

Thinly slice the tenderloin. Pour veal syrup on the plate from the middle toward 12 o'clock and place the sliced tenderloin on top in a fan shape. Serve a quenelle (see glossary) of wasabi potatoes at 2 o'clock. At 10 o'clock, place the vegetable timbale. Add a long line of the Dijon emulsion and garnish the plate with an edible flower, a Yukon gold potato crisp and a fresh herb sprig.

Serves 6

ASIAN STYLE DUCK

Tavern in the Park, Winnipeg, MB

This dish is an example of Chef Joe Dokuchie's willingness to experiment. The Canadian flavours of maple syrup and molasses season the duck to perfection. Use duck fat for roasting if it is available — it is extremely flavourful.

4 Muscovy duck legs (chicken legs can be substituted)
duck fat (or vegetable oil) to cover

Marinade

½ cup (125 mL) maple syrup
¼ cup (60 mL) molasses
½ cup (125 mL) brown sugar
1 stalk celery, diced
1 medium carrot, diced
1 onion, diced
1 tbsp (15 mL) minced ginger
7 cloves garlic, minced
2 tbsp (30 mL) salt
¼ cup (60 mL) chopped coriander
1 tsp (5 mL) crushed black peppercorns
1 tbsp (15 mL) marsala wine
1 tbsp (15 mL) sesame oil
¼ cup (60 mL) soy sauce

Combine marinade ingredients in a bowl. Add duck legs and marinate overnight. Remove legs from marinade, place in a heavy roaster and cover with duck fat or vegetable oil. Place in a 260°F (125°C) oven for 3 hours, then remove legs and cool. When ready to serve, heat legs in a 400°F (200°C) oven on a baking sheet lined with parchment until skin is crispy.

Serve on a bed of basmati rice with lightly sautéed greens of your choice.

Serves 4

TOMATO AND MOLASSES-BRAISED LAMB SHANKS

Café Brio, Victoria, BC

Rumour has it that this is one of the most popular menu items on the menu at Café Brio. Chef Greg Hayes suggests a salad for starters, as the lamb is quite rich, especially if served with a creamy polenta — and for dessert, a nice local tart topped with whipped cream. The perfect wine to pair with the lamb would be a Meritage-style red from British Columbia, or for a lighter taste a British Columbian Pinot Noir.

4 lamb shanks
4 tbsp (60 mL) olive oil
5 cups (1.25 L) thinly sliced fennel (anise)
1 onion, thinly sliced
1 celery stick, thinly sliced
1 lemon, halved
½ head of garlic (5 cloves)
1 rosemary sprig
1 bay leaf
1 24-oz (672 g) can of diced tomatoes
4 tbsp (60 mL) fancy molasses
1 cup (250 mL) white wine
stock to cover

In an ovenproof Dutch oven or similar dish, brown lamb shanks in olive oil over medium heat until golden brown, about 5 to 10 minutes. Remove lamb from pan and add vegetables and herbs, then sweat them for 5 to 10 minutes until lightly caramelized. Add tomatoes and molasses and deglaze pan with white wine. Replace lamb in the pan and cover with stock or water. Cover and bring to a boil, then place in a 300°F (150°C) oven for 3 hours, until lamb is very tender. Remove lamb and vegetables to a serving platter and keep warm. Place sauce back on a high heat and reduce by about one-half, until it is syrupy. Spoon sauce over lamb and serve with either creamy polenta or mashed potatoes.

Serves 4

PULLED PORK SANDWICH WITH MOLASSES BARBECUE SAUCE

Joy Bistro, Toronto, ON

This delicious, hearty sandwich is typical of the flavourful and extravagant tastes created by Chef Bryan Burke. The spices rubbed into the pork and allowing it to marinate for 36 hours enhance the tenderness and jolt your taste buds. Top this all off with fresh barbeque sauce and you will never want pork any other way. A culinary treat for any time of the day or night and a guaranteed tasty tradition for your kitchen, once you have tried this delicious recipe.

Pulled Pork

5 lb (2.25 kg) boneless pork shoulder
1 tsp (5 mL) cinnamon
2 tsp (10 mL) smoky paprika
2 tsp (10 mL) garlic powder
1 tsp (5 mL) ginger powder
½ tsp (2 mL) ground allspice
2 tsp (10 mL) chili powder
2 tsp (10 mL) mustard powder
1 tsp (5 mL) black pepper
2 ½ tbsp (37 mL) kosher salt
1 ½ cups (375 mL) molasses
2 large white onions
4 tbsp (60 mL) cooking oil
2 cans dark beer

Mix all the dry spices together and vigorously rub pork shoulder. Pour molasses over pork to coat all the meat. Cover and let marinate in the refrigerator for 36 hours. In a hot dutch oven add 4 tbsp (60 ml) cooking oil and brown all sides of pork shoulder. Add onions and beer. Cover and place in an oven at 275°F (135°C) for about 4 hours, or until the meat is falling apart.

Barbecue Sauce

2 white onions
2 x 28-oz cans (840 mL) plum tomatoes
3 cloves garlic
1 tbsp (15 mL) fresh ginger
2 sprigs fresh thyme
1 tbsp (60 mL) Dijon mustard
1 Granny Smith apple, sliced
1 can of dark beer
1 cup (250 mL) molasses
¼ cup (60 mL) apple cider vinegar
1 bay leaf
salt and pepper, to taste

Slice onions in half and char on barbecue until black. Put all ingredients in a pot and simmer over low heat for 45 minutes. Season to taste with salt and pepper and press through a strainer.

To serve, shred the cooked pork with two forks. Mix pork with enough barbecue sauce to make it sloppy and moist. Warm the pork mixture and serve in a crusty bun.

Serves 6 to 8

BEEF STEW WITH DARK ALE AND MOLASSES

Zest, Regina, SK

This all-time rib-sticking favourite will sooth you and take you directly to your comfort zone. Chef Rob Fuller suggests soaking up every last bit of goodness in the delicious broth with thick chunks of multigrain bread.

10 ½ oz (300 g) double-smoked bacon, cut into ¾ x ½ inch (2 x 1.25 cm) pieces

3 lb (1350 g) chuck beef, cut into ¾ inch (2 cm) cubes

2 tbsp (30 mL) all-purpose flour

1 tbsp (15 mL) salt

1 tsp (5 mL) ground black pepper

4 tbsp (60 mL) vegetable oil

2 large onions, cut into wedges

2 tbsp (30 mL) mushrooms, quartered

4 large carrots, largely diced

2 stalks celery, largely diced

4 cloves garlic, minced

1 bottle dark beer

1 tsp (5 mL) mustard seeds

coarse salt and cracked black pepper, to taste

4 tbsp (60 mL) molasses

3 cups (500 mL) beef stock

4 large potatoes, peeled, lightly parboiled and largely diced

Heat a Dutch Oven or medium stock pot over high heat and add bacon. Render the fat and cook until bacon is crispy, about 7 minutes. Remove bacon, drain and reserve. Coat beef with flour, salt and pepper and brown in the bacon fat on all sides. Remove from pot and reserve.

Using the same pot, reduce the heat to medium and add vegetable oil. Add onion, mushrooms, carrots, celery and garlic. Use a splash of beer to deglaze the pot, loosening all the brown bits sticking to the bottom of the pot. Sauté vegetables for 4 minutes or until the vegetables brown and begin to soften. Add mustard seeds and salt and pepper. Return bacon and beef to the pot. Add remaining beer, molasses and stock and bring to a boil. Reduce the heat and simmer for 10 minutes. Place in an oven at 350°F (180°C) for 75 minutes, then carefully add potatoes and cook for another 45 minutes.

Serves 6

SWEET ENDINGS

Our first-class chefs have saved the best for last with these perfect grand finales. There are spectacular desserts here for anyone, whether they have a discerning palate or simply a sweet tooth.

Desserts can be old-time favourites such as Sticky Date Pudding with Molasses Caramel Sauce, or more elegant and delicate as we find with Sake Molasses Sabayon.

And for a special occasion, you might like to outdo yourself with Coconut and Molasses Ice Cream Sandwiches or Phyllo with Caramelized Apples and Molasses Custard.

STICKY DATE PUDDING WITH MOLASSES CARAMEL SAUCE

Aqua Restaurant, St. John's, NL

Chef Mark McCrowe takes a daring approach to dishes, with a unique international flair. This dark and delicious pudding offers the perfect sweet ending to any meal. The delightful creamy topping adds a smooth and tasty contrast. It begs to be served with vanilla ice cream, accompanied by a hot beverage, and is perfect for leftovers.

Pudding

9 oz (250 g) pitted dates, roughly chopped
1 tsp (5 mL) soda water
1 ½ cups (375 mL) boiling water
4 ½ oz (125 g) unsalted butter, at room temperature
1 cup (250 mL) molasses
1 tsp (5 mL) vanilla extract
2 eggs
1 ¾ cups (440 mL) self-raising flour, sifted

Preheat oven to 350°F (180°C) and butter a 10 x 12 in (25 x 30 cm) cake pan. Place dates, soda water and boiling water in a bowl and let stand for about 20 minutes. In a mixer cream the butter, molasses and vanilla together until pale and fluffy. Add eggs, one at a time, and incorporate. Fold in flour and, using a rubber spatula, fold in date mixture until just combined. Spoon into cake pan and bake for about 30 to 35 minutes, until a toothpick comes out clean when poked in the centre. Turn out cake onto a plate or serving platter.

Sauce

1 cup (250 mL) molasses
1 cup (250 mL) whipping cream (35% m.f.)
¼ tsp (1 mL) vanilla extract
1 tbsp (15 mL) unsalted butter

Combine all ingredients in a saucepan and bring to a boil on medium heat. Reduce heat and simmer until thick (about 3 minutes).

Pour sauce over pudding just before serving.

Serves 8

PHYLLO WITH CARAMELIZED APPLES AND MOLASSES CUSTARD

Inn at St. Peters, St. Peters Bay, PEI

Chef Brad Richard stacks one sweet treat after another in this many layered delightful dessert. There are several steps, but it is worth the effort as it makes a stupendous "grande finale" to any special meal. This recipe will amaze your guests and send them home smiling.

Phyllo Squares

½ cup (125 mL) sugar
1 cup (250 mL) toasted walnuts
1 package frozen phyllo pastry
1 ½ cups (375 mL) clarified butter*

*To clarify butter: Melt butter in a saucepan over medium heat until milk solids separate. Remove milk solids. Remaining liquid is clarified butter and will not burn.

In a heavy-bottomed sauce pan, add sugar and a couple of drops of water and place over medium-high heat. Let sugar caramelize into a deep golden colour. Add toasted walnuts and spread onto a cookie sheet to cool. When cooled, use a food processor to chop nuts into a coarse mixture. On a greased cookie sheet, lay out one sheet of phyllo, brush lightly with clarified butter and sprinkle with the walnut praline. Place another sheet of phyllo over the top and repeat until you have three layers. Cut into 2 ½ x 4 ½ inch (6.25 x 11.25 cm) rectangles and toast in a 350°F (180°C) oven until golden brown.

Caramelized Apples

4 Granny Smith apples
1 tbsp (15 mL) canola oil
½ cup (125 mL) brown sugar
2 tbsp (30 mL) butter

Peel and core apples and slice into ½ in (1.25 cm) rings. Heat a pan that is large enough to accommodate all the slices. Add canola oil and sear apples until they start to brown. Add sugar and butter to the pan. Let sugar start to caramelize, then place in a 350°F (180°C) oven for about 10 to 15 minutes, or until the apples start to look caramelized and transparent, but not overcooked and mushy. The apples can be reheated to serve later.

Ginger English Cream

1 cup (250 mL) cream
¼ cup (60 mL) sugar
1 x 3 in (7.5 cm) piece fresh ginger, peeled and sliced
3 egg yolks

Heat cream, sugar and ginger to a simmer. Let ginger steep for 4 or 5 minutes, then whisk cream into egg yolks, slowly so that they do not cook. Strain into a metal bowl, place over a double boiler and stir constantly until liquid coats the back of a wooden spoon. Chill.

Molasses Custard

1 cup (250 mL) cream
½ cup (125mL) molasses
3 egg yolks

Place cream and molasses into a sauce pot, bring to a boil and cool slightly. Slowly whisk the mixture into egg yolks. Strain through a fine-mesh strainer. Pour into a baking dish and place dish in a larger pan filled with enough water to come halfway up the baking dish. Cook in a 300°F (150°C) oven for 30 to 60 minutes, or until the custard sets. Pass through a tamis (a stainless steel sieve available in various sizes) and place into a piping bag fitted with a straight, wide tip.

To assemble, pour ginger cream into the centre of a large dinner plate. Place a rectangle of phyllo over the sauce. On top of the phyllo, place two warm caramelized apple rings, then another rectangle of phyllo. Pipe the molasses custard to cover the second phyllo rectangle, and top with the final phyllo rectangle. Place a scoop of pure vanilla ice cream on the centre of the dessert and garnish with a sprig of mint. Whipped cream can be used in place of ice cream and sprinkled with toasted or candied walnuts.

Serves 4

SAKE MOLASSES SABAYON

Wild Tangerine, Edmonton, AB

Chef Judy Wu has added a special touch of distinction to this scrumptious sabayon, which she has perked up with the surprise flavours of sake and molasses. So simple, yet so perfect.

>   4 large egg yolks
>   2 tbsp (30 mL) molasses
>   2 tbsp (30 mL) sugar
>   6 tbsp (90 mL) sake wine

Heat up a double boiler. Whip egg yolks, molasses and sugar for 1 minute in a dry stainless bowl. Add sake promptly and add mixture to double boiler. Whip mixture vigorously until sabayon coats the back of a spoon.

Yields 4 small compotes

WARM GINGERBREAD AND PUMPKIN MOLASSES ICE CREAM

Wickaninnish Inn's Pointe Restaurant, Tofino, BC

Chef de Cuisine Tim Cuff has a knack for combining creativity and comfort in everything he prepares. As if this moist and delicious gingerbread with its pumpkin molasses ice cream did not stand apart, along comes an extra-special pumpkin compote to complete the ensemble.

Gingerbread

½ tbsp (7 mL) baking soda
3 cups (750 mL) boiling water
2 cups (500 mL) molasses
½ lb (225g) butter
2 cups (500 mL) brown sugar
2 ¾ cups (875 mL) unsifted flour
1 tbsp (15 mL) ground ginger
2 tsp (10 mL) ground cinnamon
½ tsp (2 mL) ground cloves
2 tbsp (30 mL) baking powder
2 eggs

Mix baking soda, water and molasses together and let cool. Cream the butter and sugar together. Sift flour, spices and baking powder together. Slowly add eggs to butter mixture. Add sifted flour mixture to molasses mixture and combine with the butter mixture. Batter will be wet. Pour into two banana-bread-sized greased and floured loaf pans (1 inch [2.5 cm] below the top of the pan to allow for rising) and bake at 350°F (180°C) for approximately 40 minutes, or until done.

Ice Cream

2 cups (500 mL) milk
¼ vanilla bean, scraped
5 tbsp (75 mL) molasses
¼ tsp (1 mL) ground cinnamon
9 egg yolks
6 tbsp (90 mL) sugar
1 cup (250 mL) cream
3 tbsp (45 mL) honey
½ cup (125 mL) pumpkin purée

Bring milk to a boil with vanilla, molasses and cinnamon. Whisk yolks and sugar together. Add boiled milk to yolks and cook until thickened. Quickly add cream, honey and pumpkin. Strain and cool over ice. Freeze in an ice cream machine.

Yields 5 cups (1.25 litres)

Pumpkin Compote

1 cup (250 mL) diced pumpkin
½ cup (125 mL) raisins
2 cups (500 mL) boiled water
1 tbsp (15 mL) molasses
13 tbsp (200 mL) apple juice

Soak raisins in boiled water to plump them up. Add diced pumpkin, molasses and apple juice and cook until pumpkin is soft but still retains its shape and apple juice is reduced. Stir in drained plump raisins and serve in side dish. Serve a slice of the warm gingerbread with a little of the compote and a scoop of the ice cream.

Makes 10 to 12 generous servings

MOLASSES MOUSSE WITH BRAISED RHUBARB AND RUM CARAMEL

Magnum and Steins, St. John's, NL

Chef Antonio Esperanza has done it again with this fabulous combination, which is bursting with vibrant and stimulating flavours and can be made the day before a dinner party. The ramekins can be decorated to suit your decor and your guests can add as much of the ravishing rum sauce as they wish. You are guaranteed to be asked for your recipe.

Braised Rhubarb

1 lb (450 g) fresh rhubarb, cut into ½ in (1 cm) pieces, or individually quick-frozen (IQF) rhubarb pieces
2 Granny Smith apples, peeled, cored and dried
2 tbsp (30 mL) unsalted butter
4 tbsp (60 mL) semi-sweet white wine (e.g. Riesling or Gewürztraminer)
4 tbsp (60 mL) molasses
1 tsp (5 mL) vanilla extract
1 tsp (5 mL) ground cinnamon
pinch ground nutmeg
2 tbsp (30 mL) lemon juice

Sauté rhubarb and apple in butter until they just begin to soften. Add wine and simmer until it has reduced by half. Add remaining ingredients and continue to simmer on low heat until rhubarb becomes quite tender. Remove from heat and let cool to room temperature. The cooked rhubarb can be stored in a refrigerator for up to 8 days.

Molasses Mousse

4 egg yolks
½ cup (125 mL) fancy molasses
1 ¼ cups (310 mL) whipping cream
½ tbsp (7 mL) powdered gelatin

In a stainless steel bowl, whip egg yolks and molasses together and place over a simmering pot of water, creating a double boiler. Stir constantly until mixture thickens and forms ribbons as you pull away the whisk or spoon. Be careful not to overcook the egg yolk mixture, or it will curdle — you are looking for a smooth, light mixture. Remove from heat and set aside. In a well-chilled bowl, whip cream into firm peaks and refrigerate. Dissolve gelatin with a few drops of water in a heatproof ramekin. Wait until gelatin blooms, then place in a shallow sauté pan and fill the pan with water until it comes halfway up the ramekin. Place on medium-high heat, stirring occasionally. Once in liquid form, add gelatin to egg yolks and molasses. Fold this mixture into the whipped cream. Be sure the mixture is completely uniform. Divide the mousse into 4 to 6 8-oz (225-g) individual ramekins and refrigerate.

Rum Caramel

¼ cup (60 mL) white sugar

2 tbsp (30 mL) water

2 tbsp (30 mL) molasses

¼ cup (60 mL) whipping cream

1 tsp (5 mL) vanilla extract

4 tbsp (60 mL) dark rum

2 tbsp (30 mL) unsalted butter

In a heavy frying pan on medium heat, add sugar, water and molasses. Bring to a boil and watch carefully to ensure that it doesn't burn. Stir evenly but carefully and bring mixture to the colour of mahogany. Add cream and stir well, as the cream will cool the mix and might harden. Keep stirring and any lumps will break down. Remove from heat and add vanilla, rum and butter. Mix completely and let stand.

To assemble, place the ramekins in very hot water and turn them out onto dessert plates. Spoon braised rhubarb over the mousse, either warmed or at room temperature, and drizzle with rum caramel sauce.

Serves 4 to 6

COCONUT AND MOLASSES ICE CREAM SANDWICHES

Restaurant Le Saint-Amour, Quebec, QC

Chefs Éric Lessard and Jean-Luc and Frédéric Boulay feel this dessert is well worth the effort and will delight your dinner guests. The ice cream itself is so exquisite that I also serve it on it's own in a crystal dessert dish. The beauty of these ice cream sandwiches is that they can be made ahead and kept in the freezer. Some truffles served on the side make an ideal complement. The sandwiches are nice served with chocolate wafers as well. You can be as inventive as you like with this recipe.

Crunchy Molasses and Ginger Cookie

    1 ½ cup (375 mL) unsifted white flour
    1 tbsp (15 mL) fresh ginger
    1 tsp (5 mL) cinnamon
    ½ tsp (2 mL) salt
    ½ cup (125 mL) unsalted butter
    5 tbsp (75 mL) fancy molasses

Sift and mix all dry ingredients and set aside. Cream butter and slowly add molasses while continuing to mix. Gradually incorporate dry ingredients with butter and molasses mixture. Cool for 1 hour and press down to ⅛ inch (3 mm) thickness directly on a lightly floured silicon baking sheet. Cut with a 2 ½ inch (6 cm) cookie cutter. (This size works well as a dessert, however, if you want a bite-sized treat, use a 2 inch [3 cm] cookie cutter.) Bake at 315°F (160°C) until cookies are browned (5 to 7 minutes). Cool on a wire rack.

Ice Cream

    ½ cup (125 mL) shredded coconut
    2 tbsp (30 mL) molasses
    2 cups (500 mL) slightly softened vanilla ice cream

Blend all ingredients and while still soft, add a small scoop to the middle of a cooled cookie, add the top cookie and press down.

Store in the freezer on a baking sheet until ready to serve.

Makes 6 sandwiches

MOLASSES OATMEAL RAISIN COOKIES

Kamloops Catering (Culinary Provider)
Rocky Mountaineer Railway, Kamloops, BC

These soft and delicious cookies get rave reviews from guests on the Rocky Mountaineer Railway. We are delighted Kamloops Catering shared their recipe so now you can make these cookies at home and enjoy receiving your own compliments.

1 cup (250 mL) granulated sugar
½ cup (125 mL) shortening
1 egg
½ cup (125 mL) molasses
2 cups (500 mL) sifted flour
1 tsp (5 mL) salt
1 ½ tsp (7 mL) baking soda
1 tsp (5 mL) vanilla extract
1 cup (250 mL) quick-cooking oats
1 to 1 ½ cups (250 to 375 mL) raisins
1 cup (250 mL) chopped walnuts or pecans (optional)

Cream the sugar and shortening together in a large mixing bowl. Add egg and molasses. Beat well and add flour, salt and baking soda. Mix well, add vanilla and stir in oatmeal, raisins and nuts (if using). Drop batter from a teaspoon onto a greased baking sheet. Bake cookies at 375°F (190°C) for 10 to 12 minutes, until done.

Makes about 48 cookies

LAVENDER CITRUS GINGER SNAPS

Rossmount Inn, St. Andrews, NB

Chef Mark Shafransky talks passionately about this wonderfully flavourful cookie. The pink pepper and lavender add a kick that will earn this recipe a permanent place in your "favourites" collection. You can be as inventive as you like with the spices — try using equal amounts of cloves or nutmeg and also some sesame seeds or coriander, for instance. These cookies are crunchy and savoury and perfect with your favourite tea.

½ lb (225 g) unsalted butter, softened
¾ cup (185 mL) brown sugar
¾ cup (185 mL) white sugar
½ tsp (2 mL) vanilla
3 tbsp (45 mL) molasses
2 eggs
3 cups (750 mL) flour
2 ½ tsp (12 mL) baking soda
½ tsp (2 mL) salt
2 ½ tsp (12 mL) cinnamon
½ tsp (2 mL) cloves
½ tsp (2 mL) ground ginger
2 ½ tsp (12 mL) candied ginger, minced
½ tsp (2 mL) pink peppercorns, finely ground
½ tsp (2 mL) ground lavender flowers
½ tsp (2 mL) orange zest (lemon or lime zest can be substituted)

Cream the butter, sugars and vanilla with a paddle attachment until smooth. Drizzle in molasses on slow speed and add eggs, one at a time, on medium speed. In a separate bowl, mix flour, baking soda and salt, followed by all the other dry ingredients. With mixer on slow, add flour mixture to wet ingredients until dough is just formed. This makes a beautiful sticky dough — very soft and supple. Cover and refrigerate for 2-3 hours (or overnight). Preheat the oven to 350°F (180°C). Roll out dough on a silicone pad* to ¼" (6-mm) thickness and cut into rounds. Cook in oven until golden brown. Flip off immediately and cool on a rack.

*Silicone pads are a wonderful invention for the kitchen. There is no need to grease them or use parchment paper. They retain their heat and last for a very long time.

Makes 36 to 48 cookies

MOLASSES AND MAPLE CRÈME BRÛLÉE

Opera Bistro, Saint John, NB

You are guaranteed to leave the table with the senses fully satisfied after this exquisite dessert. It is the ultimate indulgence after any meal. Chef Margaret Begner enriches this crème brûlée with the "sweet sisters," molasses and maple syrup. No one can resist the crunchy caramelized topping followed by the delightfully creamy custard below. For convenience the custard can be made 2 to 3 days before serving. Caramelize the tops just before your guests arrive using a chef's blow torch.

2 cups (500 mL) whipping cream
6 egg yolks
1 tbsp (15 mL) sugar
2 tbsp (30 mL) maple syrup
2 tbsp (30 mL) molasses
½ cup (125 mL) sugar to sprinkle on individual ramekins

Boil whipping cream. Combine egg yolks, sugar, maple syrup and molasses. Pour hot cream over egg mixture. Fill a pan with hot water. Divide custard into 6 ramekins and place in pan. Bake for 45 minutes at 300°F (150°C). Let cool. Sprinkle with sugar and then caramelize the sugar with a blowtorch.

Serves 6

SWEET AND SPICY NUTS

Gabrieau's Bistro, Antigonish, NS

These sweet and spicy nuts have many uses and are a crowd pleaser for all ages. They taste fantastic and are easy to prepare. Chef Mark Gabrieau uses them in salads, but they also work well on ice cream, as a party snack or as a hostess or Christmas gift. If you like extra spice you can sprinkle them with spices of your choice (cayenne pepper, Cajun spice or hot paprika, for example) before baking.

> 3 cups (750 mL) walnuts (pecans or almonds can also be used)
> 2 to 3 cups (500 to 750 mL) molasses
> Cajun spice, cayenne pepper, hot or smoked paprika to taste (optional)

Preheat oven to 350°F (180°C). In a heavy-bottomed saucepan, cover the nuts completely with molasses and bring to a boil for 3 minutes, taking care not to burn the mixture. Thoroughly drain the nuts in a colander and spread them out on a parchment-lined cookie sheet. Sprinkle with spices, to taste, if desired. Cook in oven for 7 to 8 minutes (or until molasses becomes slightly frothy) then cool. Break the nuts apart and store them in a covered glass container.

Yields 3 cups (750 mL)

SAUCES, DRESSINGS AND MARINADES

Sauces and marinades provide that extra-special sizzle of taste for your table or grill, increasing the flavour and colour of any dish you choose to use them with.

From Rum Banana Chutney to Cognac and Molasses-Compound Butter to Mission Figs and Molasses Compote, all the recipes in this section will accessorize and bring to life the other items on your menu. They are guaranteed to add an unforgettable touch to your cooking.

MOLASSES AND LEMON VINAIGRETTE WITH THYME

Rothesay Netherwood School, Rothesay, NB

Chef Steve Cyr is a wizard with the ingredients of this delightful vinaigrette. The flavour of finely chopped mint combined with the sweetness of the molasses and the tangy-sweet spirit of the balsamic vinegar make this versatile homemade dressing an excellent companion for salads, lamb, pork or fish.

    1 cup (250 mL) olive oil
    1 cup (250 mL) balsamic vinegar
    ½ cup (125 mL) molasses
    ¼ cup (60 mL) lemon juice
    1 tbsp (15 mL) finely chopped mint
    1 tbsp (15 mL) cracked pink peppercorns
    salt to taste

Combine all ingredients. The dressing can be covered and stored for several days in your favourite glass container, ready to set directly on the table.

Yields 3 cups (750 mL)

THAI SOY PEANUT MOLASSES DRESSING

John's Prime Rib and Steakhouse, Saskatoon, SK

Chef Andrew Shedd's dressing adds zip to many an ordinary dish. It is equally delicious on salads or with chicken, beef or fish.

   2 tbsp (30 mL) garlic purée
   ¼ cup (60 mL) sesame oil
   1 tbsp (15 mL) ground ginger
   2 tbsp (30 mL) chilli flakes
   1 cup (250 mL) rice wine vinegar
   ¼ cup (60 mL) soy sauce
   ¼ cup (60 mL) sugar
   ¼ cup (60 mL) peanut butter
   ¼ cup (60 mL) molasses
   1 cup (250 mL) water

Sauté garlic in sesame oil, then add ginger, chili, vinegar, soy sauce and sugar. Simmer for 5 minutes. Add peanut butter and molasses in stages. Bring to a boil, reduce to a simmer and add water in stages for desired consistency. Simmer for approximately 20 minutes. Remove from heat and strain if desired. Cool and serve on Thai salads with chicken or beef.

Yields 3 cups (750 mL)

BARBECUE SAUCE

Shadow Lawn Inn, Rothesay, NB

What makes Chef Darren Bennett's barbecue sauce different is the addition of strong coffee and liquid smoke. It will certainly add zing to your grill.

2 tbsp (30 mL) fresh garlic, finely chopped
2 tbsp (30 mL) fresh ginger, finely chopped
4 tbsp (60 mL) salt
1 tbsp (15 mL) cloves
1 ½ tsp (7 mL) peppercorns
2 tbsp (30 mL) allspice
1 tsp (5 mL) cayenne pepper
3 ¾ cups (940 mL) brown sugar
2 ½ cups (600 mL) red wine vinegar
¼ cup (60 mL) Dijon mustard
¾ cup (185 mL) red wine
1 cup (250 mL) molasses
1 cup (250 mL) strong coffee
2 tsp (10 mL) liquid smoke
11 lb (5 kg) plum (Roma) tomatoes

Bring all ingredients except tomatoes to a boil. Add tomatoes and turn heat down to a simmer for about 2 hours or until done. Reduce mixture to the consistency of jam, stirring occasionally. Purée in a food processor. This recipe makes a large quantity of absolutely delicious barbeque sauce which is perfect for gift giving. Simply bottle while still hot in sterilized mason jars. It keeps well for up to a month in the refrigerator after opening but is guaranteed to be used up quickly.

Yields 6 litres (0.22 gallons)

RUM BANANA CHUTNEY

Beatty & the Beastro, Saint John, NB

Chef Helen Buck is a familiar presence at Beatty & The Beastro, but she is also a regular CBC Radio guest, sharing her unending words of wisdom about all kinds of food and drink.

She says that this chutney makes an unusual condiment to serve with roasted or grilled meats, but it is particularly nice with baked ham, excellent with spicy jerk-style chicken and an interesting complement to curries.

    4 large, ripe bananas, peeled and sliced
    2 cups (500 mL) chopped onions
    2 cloves garlic, minced
    ½ cup (125 mL chopped) pitted dates
    ½ cup (125 mL) chopped figs or raisins
    1 large apple, peeled, cored and chopped
    1 cup (250 mL) white wine (or cider) vinegar
    ½ tsp (125 mL) ground cloves
    ¼ cup (60 mL) finely chopped candied ginger
    1 tsp (5 mL) allspice
    ½ cup (125 mL) molasses
    juice of 1 lemon
    ¼ cup (125 mL) dark rum

In a heavy stainless steel pot, combine all ingredients except rum. Bring to a boil, lower heat and simmer, uncovered, for 2 hours, stirring occasionally. Remove from heat, stir in rum and cool. Keep refrigerated.

Yields 5 to 6 cups (1.25 to 1.5 L)

COGNAC AND MOLASSES-COMPOUND BUTTER

Oscar's, Barrie, ON

Chef Rachael Whitman says that this butter is a real treat to keep in the refrigerator and use on steak or fish, in potatoes, or in whatever else inspires you. Toasting the spices will intensify the flavour.

1 shallot, finely diced
1 tsp (5 mL) puréed garlic
1 tbsp (15 mL) oil
l tbsp (15 mL) butter
1 pinch each of curry, allspice and pink pepper (all ground)
½ cup (125 mL) white cooking wine
2 tbsp (30 mL) molasses
½ cup (125 mL) whipping cream (35% m.f.)
2 tbsp (30 mL) cognac
salt and pepper
2 dashes each, Tabasco and Worcestershire sauces
2 tbsp (30 mL) fresh lemon juice
1 lb (450 g) sweet butter, at room temperature
1 large egg

In a saucepan, start to sweat shallot and garlic with butter and oil. Cook on low heat until transparent so as not to impart any color to the finished dish. Add curry, allspice and pink pepper (keep a watchful eye to prevent browning or burning) and deglaze with white wine. Reduce until there is no liquid left in the pan. Add molasses and let it bubble in the pan for 10 seconds to caramelize some of the sugar. Add cream and reduce by 80 percent, then add cognac and let simmer for another 10 seconds. Stir constantly at this point to avoid everything sticking to the bottom of the pan. Remove from heat, cool slightly and season with salt, pepper, Tabasco and Worcestershire sauces and lemon juice.

In a large bowl, use a whisk or a mixer with whisk attachment to work the sweet butter until it is soft and spreadable in consistency. Add cream reduction and egg, and mix into butter until evenly distributed. Line a terrine mould (a glazed earthenware dish with a vertical side and a tightly fitting lid) with plastic wrap and add butter. Store in the freezer and use as needed by slicing off desired amounts.

The desired shape of the pats is cylindrical and 1 inch (2.5 cm) in diameter, so that a pat can be served as an individual portion on top of steaks, corn on the cob or pork tenderloin. The butter may also be piped into other shapes and frozen for later use. The temperature must be cool enough so that the butter will pour out of the piping bag, but warm enough so that it does not stick in the bag. Freeze in a covered container separated with wax or parchment paper for later use.

Yields 30 to 40 individual portions

PASTRAMI CURE

The Willow on Wascana, Regina, SK

Chef Maurice Mathieu uses this cure for turkey, pork tenderloin or trout. The longer you leave the meat or fish to cure, the more the flavours will build.

1 cup (250 mL) molasses
1 tbsp (15 mL) cayenne
2 tbsp (30 mL) coriander seed
1 tbsp (15 mL) black pepper, freshly ground
1 tbsp (15 mL) sea salt
1 tbsp (15 mL) mustard seed
¼ tsp (1 mL) smoked paprika
1 tbsp (15 mL) lemon zest or powder

Mix all ingredients together into a soft wet cure. Pour mixture over meat or fish and let sit for 2 to 3 hours. Hot smoke product until it is cooked all the way through. If you don't have a hot smoker, place smoking chips in a roasting pan with a wire rack on top. Cover the meat or fish with aluminum foil and you have a ready-made smoker.

MUSTARD BOURBON MARINADE

The Bison Mountain Bistro, Banff, AB

According to Chef Ryan Rivard, this marinade is the perfect choice to infuse flavour into chicken, pork, beef or bison. It cannot be beaten, and is also sold by the bottle at the Bison Mountain Bistro.

2 cups (500 mL) cider vinegar
1 cup (250 mL) molasses
2 ½ cups (625 mL) grainy mustard
6 tbsp (90 mL) hot sauce
5 tbsp (75 mL) Worcestershire sauce
1 cup (250 mL) bourbon
2 cups (500 mL) canola oil
24 cloves garlic (puréed with a little oil)
4 bay leaves
6 tbsp (90 mL) ground basil

Combine all ingredients, and use to marinate the meat of your choice.

Yields 8 cups (2 L)

MOLASSES DRESSING

The Willow on Wascana, Regina, SK

*This fabulous dressing, created by Chef Maurice
Mathieu, is great on meats, chicken and fish. It also
makes a great sandwich spread. Further thinned, it
goes well with greens.*

- 1 clove garlic, minced
- 1 small shallot, minced
- ¼ cup (60 mL) molasses
- ½ tsp (2 mL) mustard
- 1 tbsp (15 mL) salt
- 1 tbsp (15 mL) pepper
- ¾ cup (180 mL) canola oil
- 1 tbsp (15 mL) dark rum

In a bowl, mix all ingredients thoroughly except rum
and oil. Incorporate oil slowly so that the mixture
emulsifies like a mayonnaise. Add rum to finish and to
thin dressing.

Yields 1 cup (250 mL)

MISSION FIGS AND MOLASSES COMPOTE

Barking Fish Tavern, Saskatoon, SK

This fantastic compote is warm and rich in flavour, with the combined textures of figs and mushrooms. Chef Jean François Dionne says this compote is perfect for either fish or meat, and will thrill the taste buds.

2 shallots, minced
2 portobello mushrooms, minced
½ lb (225 g) dry mission figs, sliced
3 garlic cloves, minced
2 tbsp (30 mL) olive oil
1 fresh mango, julienned
2 tbsp (30 mL) rice wine vinegar
1 tsp (5 mL) chili flakes
1 cup (250 mL) apple juice
¼ cup (60 mL) red wine vinegar
5 tbsp (75 mL) blackstrap molasses
1 tbsp (15 mL) siracha hot sauce (available at any Chinese grocery store or in the import section at your supermarket)

In a medium-sized pot over medium heat, sweat shallots, mushrooms, figs and garlic in olive oil for 4 to 5 minutes. Add remaining ingredients and simmer slowly until most of the liquid has evaporated. Serve hot or at room temperature.

Yields 2 cups (500 mL)

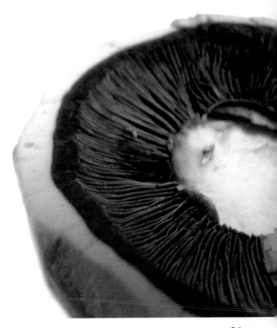

SASKATOON BERRY AND MOLASSES VINAIGRETTE

John's Prime Rib and Steakhouse, Saskatoon, SK

This vinaigrette can be used on a salad topped with cooked salmon, and also on fish or chicken. The flavours are luscious and tart and guaranteed to add a bold and lively extra touch.

4 cups (1 L) Saskatoon berries (cranberries can be substituted)
1 ½ cups (375 mL) sugar
¼ cup (60 mL) lemon juice
4 cups (1 L) extra virgin olive oil
½ cup (125 mL) apple cider vinegar
1 cup (250 mL) molasses
1 cup (250 mL) Saskatoon berry juice (cranberry juice can be substituted)
2 tbsp (30 mL) Dijon mustard

Simmer berries, sugar and lemon juice over medium low heat until berries start to burst. More sugar can be added to dressing if preferred. Purée and strain if desired, then cool. Whisk remaining ingredients together, add to the berry purée and let stand at room temperature for at least 1 hour before using.

Yields 8 cups (2 litres)

MOLASSES AND HORSERADISH VINAIGRETTE

Shadow Lawn Inn, Rothesay, NB

*Chef Darren Bennett uses this vinaigrette for salads, as
a marinade for salmon, and as a sauce with any kind
of meat. It goes exceptionally well with smoked
salmon. So easy to prepare, it adds that little extra
touch of homemade goodness.*

  3 tbsp (45 mL) prepared horseradish
  1 tbsp (15 mL) Dijon mustard
  ⅓ cup (75 mL) molasses
  3 tbsp (45 mL) apple cider vinegar
  ⅔ cup (150 mL) canola oil
  1 tsp (5 mL) salt
  ½ tsp (2 mL) ground white pepper

Whisk all ingredients together, cover and refrigerate.

Yields approximately 1 cup

INDEX

INDEX

Special thanks to Michael Howell, Chef/Proprietor at Tempest World Cuisine in Wolfville, Nova Scotia, and Executive Chef at The Port Gastropub in Port Williams, Nova Scotia, for preparing and styling the recipes photographed for this book.

PHOTO CREDITS

Participating Restaurants

British Columbia
Arbutus, Brentwood Bay, BC
Bacchus, Vancouver, BC
Feenies, Vancouver, BC
Kamloop's Catering, Rocky Mountaineer Railway, Kamloops, BC
Wickaninnish Inn's Pointe Restaurant, Tofino, BC
Alberta
Capo Restaurant, Calgary, AB
La Bohème Restaurant B & B, Edmonton, AB
The Bison Mountain Bistro, Banff, AB
The Harvest Room, Edmonton, AB
Wild Tangerine, Edmonton, AB
Saskatchewan
Barking Fish Tavern, Saskatoon, SK
Cathedral Freehouse, Regina, SK
John's Prime Rib & Steakhouse, Saskatoon, SK
Mojo, Regina, SK
The Willow on Wascana, Regina, SK
Zest, Regina, SK
Manitoba
Fude, Winnipeg, MB
Tavern in the Park, Winnipeg, MB
The Dandelion Eatery, Winnipeg, MB
Ontario
Joy Bistro, Toronto, ON
Oscar's, Barrie, ON
Quebec
Aux Vivres, Montreal, QC

Garçon!, Montreal, QC
Le Bistro, Montreal, QC
Maestro S.V.P., Montreal, QC
Restaurant Le Saint-Amour, Quebec, QC
New Brunswick
Beatty & the Beastro, Saint John, NB
Opera Bistro, Saint John, NB
Personal Chef to the Lieutenant-Governor of New Brunswick, Fredericton, NB
Racines, Fredericton, NB
Rossmount Inn, St Andrews, NB
Rothesay Netherwood School, Rothesay, NB
Shadow Lawn Inn, Rothesay, NB
Saint John Ale House, Saint John, NB
Nova Scotia
Blomidon Inn, Wolfville, NS
Chez Bruno, Yarmouth, NS
Gabrieau's Bistro, Antigonish, NS
Gio, Halifax, NS
Prince Edward Island
Inn at St. Peters, St. Peters Bay, PEI
Victoria Village Inn, Victoria-by-the-Sea, PEI
Newfoundland
Aqua Restaurant, St. John's, NL
Cabot Club (Fairmont), St. John's, NL
Glynn Mill Inn, Corner Brook, NL
Magnum and Steins, St. John's, NL